Praise for

THE POWER OF INNER SPARKLE

"*The Power of Inner Sparkle* is a heartfelt collection of wisdom, courage, and inspiration. Bobbi Wilcox, along with twelve co-authors, shares powerful stories that remind us that no matter what challenges we face, the light within us is always strong enough to lead the way. This book is a beautiful testament to the power of self-love, resilience, and living a purpose-driven life. I highly recommend it."
— Jack Canfield, Coauthor of the *Chicken Soup for the Soul*® series and *The Success Principles*™

"*The Power of Inner Sparkle* isn't just a book—it's a radiant invitation to every woman who's ever forgotten how powerful she truly is. Bobbi Wilcox and her courageous co-authors have created something rare: a space where vulnerability meets victory, and every story is a spark that lights the way forward. These pages are filled with truth, heart, and the kind of soul-deep wisdom that reminds us we're never alone. If you're ready to reconnect with your light and rise with a little more grace and grit, start here."
— Patty Aubery, President, The Canfield Training Group #1 New York Times Bestselling Author, *Chicken Soup for the Working Women's Soul*

"*The Power of Inner Sparkle*" is a remarkable celebration of resilience, authenticity, and the unstoppable spirit within each of us. It shines a powerful light on the importance of empowering women to step fully into their brilliance and lead with heart, courage, and wisdom. This inspiring collection of stories reminds us that when women embrace their inner sparkle, they not only transform their own lives—they transform the world. It is an honor to support such a beautiful and meaningful work.
— Robert Rockefeller, President and Founder of R.C. Rockefeller Entertainment, Philanthropist, and Advocate for Women's Empowerment

THE POWER OF INNER SPARKLE

THE POWER OF INNER SPARKLE

12 Inspiring Stories to Ignite Your Heart & Soul

Bobbi Wilcox

Published by Heart & Soul Publishing

ISBN (paperback): 979-8-218-67403-8
ISBN (ebook): 979-8-9988284-0-9

Book design and production by www.AuthorSuccess.com

Printed in the United States of America

DEDICATION

This book is dedicated to the generations whose love, wisdom, and light have guided the past, shine brightly in the present, and inspire the future.

Each of us wrote from the heart, guided by a divine whisper that said, "I wrote this book for you." We know it's meant for you, the women ready to be seen, heard, and uplifted. We are thankful for this divinely guided gift.

CONTENTS

FOREWORD

There's something sacred about when a woman finally gets tired of dimming her light. When she decides she's done shrinking, done explaining, and ready to stand fully in her truth—even if her voice shakes, even if nobody claps. That's where her power lives.

Not pretending. Not performing. Just standing in the truth of who she is—with all her experiences, all her scars, and all her strength—and saying, "This is me. And I'm still here."

When I was asked to write the foreword for *The Power of Inner Sparkle*, I paused. Not because I wasn't honored—I was. But because I knew what this really meant. This wasn't just an introduction. It was an invitation; a responsibility to help open the door to something that's not always easy to talk about.

Because let's be real—finding your sparkle again after life has tried to snuff it out? That's no small thing.

These women—these beautiful, brave souls in this book—have walked through real stuff. The kind of stuff that doesn't just challenge you, it changes you. Trauma, heartbreak, illness, betrayal, self-doubt, silence. The women in this book have had moments where they didn't know if they'd make it through. And yet they found a way.

Not overnight. Not in a straight line. But they found it.

And that's what moved me so deeply when reading these stories. There's no sugarcoating here. Just truth. The raw, complicated, inspiring kind. Every woman in these pages said yes to being seen. Yes, to telling the truth. Yes, to shining again, not because life got easier—but because they decided *they* were worth it.

That's courage.

I've spent most of my life amplifying other people's voices—from TV talk shows to live events to virtual stages—and I've learned something important: when women share their truth, something shifts. In the room. In the reader. In the woman herself. We connect. We heal. We remember that we're not alone.

And here's the truth: we all have a sparkle. But sometimes, life dims it. We go through things. We adapt. We survive. But somewhere along the way, we forget how bright we used to be.

This book? It's a reminder.

It's a gentle nudge to reconnect with that girl inside you—the one who dreamed big, laughed loud, cried deep, and loved fully. The one who never needed permission to shine.

So, as you read these pages, don't rush. Let the stories breathe. Let them speak to the parts of you that you've kept quiet. Maybe you'll cry. Maybe you'll smile. Maybe you'll feel something stir that you haven't felt in a long time.

Whatever happens, just know this: you are not alone. You are not broken. And your sparkle? It's still there. Waiting.

Waiting for *you*.

With love, truth, and a whole lotta sparkle,

Dr. Theresa "TGo" Goss, Founder of Network of Outstanding (NOW) Honors, Power of Pink Summit, and SV Trailblazer

DISCLAIMERS

This book may contain content that is sensitive or triggering for some readers. It may include discussions of the following topics:

1. Sexual trauma

2. Substance abuse

3. Suicide trauma

4. Childhood traumas

5. Emotional or mental abuse

6. Physical abuse, domestic violence

7. Grief and loss

Chapters with trauma triggers will be marked with a disclaimer number on the Chapter Introduction page. Reader discretion is advised. If you or someone you know is affected by any of these issues, please seek support from a mental health professional or a trusted resource.

All of the people mentioned in each chapter are real, but some of the names and details have been changed to protect their privacy.

INTRODUCTION

WHY WOMEN ARE MEANT TO SPARKLE

As women, many of us have been taught to hide our light. We fear being judged, rejected, or labeled "too much." We've been conditioned to believe that letting our sparkle shine might make others uncomfortable. Perhaps we fear others' jealousy, their affection withdrawal, or that our flaws will be exposed. These fears and the persistent "not enough" messages—not pretty, thin, smart, or good enough—dim our inner light. They leave us feeling unworthy of fully stepping into our authentic selves and embracing who we are.

We often sabotage ourselves with harsh self-criticism, buying into narratives of failure: a failed marriage, business setbacks, abusive relationships, motherhood struggles, or financial hardships. These stories become evidence of supposed inadequacy. I know this because it was my story for much of my life.

As a mother and a wife, I prioritized my children's needs over mine. Many of us have been taught to do this, but over time, I've learned a profound truth: nurturing ourselves is not selfish; it's essential.

1

When we awaken to our true loving nature, we begin to see that our past choices and experiences aren't failures. They are lessons—powerful opportunities for growth, self-love, and acceptance. I've come to understand that caring for myself, just as I care for others, is a gift I give to myself and those around me.

Each of us carries a divine light within. This light—our inner sparkle—isn't meant to be hidden or diminished. It's intended to shine boldly and brightly. When we embrace this truth, we honor our authentic selves and reclaim our power.

Jamie Kern Lima beautifully says in her book *Worthy*, "It takes bravery to trust yourself even when others tell you to dim your light."

We are all meant to sparkle. We are all worthy of letting our inner light shine.

WHAT IS INNER SPARKLE?

When I began compiling this book, I asked several women to describe what *sparkle* meant to them. Their responses were as vibrant and multifaceted as the word itself: aliveness, fun, vivacity, brilliance, brightness, inner light, youthfulness, a diamond-like quality, the essence of self, bringing life to everything, shining, radiating, authenticity, and joy.

What about you? What does *sparkle* mean to you? How does it make you feel inside?

The *Merriam-Webster Dictionary* defines *sparkle* as: "to shine brightly with flashes of light" or "to be vivacious and witty." But in the context of this book, *inner sparkle* holds a much deeper meaning—it is a reflection of our loving essence.

Loving essence refers to the unconditional and authentic expression of love that resides within each of us. It is the radiant purity we see in newborn babies, the natural wonder we witness in young children, and the core of who we authentically are. In spiritual psychology, the loving essence is often described as the authentic self—a state of being where we give and receive love unconditionally.

Each of us carries a *divine sparkle*. This inner sparkle is a luminous expression of the divine light within us. It's visible in the gleam of our eyes, felt in the warmth of joy and gratitude in our hearts, and known in the clarity and wisdom of our minds. It is soulful, vibrant, energizing, and contagious—a force that uplifts, renews, and inspires everyone it touches.

Our inner sparkle shines through in our creativity, imagination, passion, and brilliance—whether expressed through art, music, mathematics, science, or any form of self-expression. It emerges in moments of courage, resilience, and personal growth, often shaped by life's challenges. It flourishes as we cultivate self-love, worthiness, and wisdom.

This inner sparkle is not just something we possess—it is who we are.

WHY I WAS CALLED TO THE SPARKLE PROJECT

I've written several books, beginning with my first self-published work, *Reconciled*, in 2016. In 2025, I co-authored *The Art of Connection: 365 Days of Abundance Quotes by Entrepreneurs, Business Owners, and Influencers*, a number-one international bestseller. Along the way, I've also written a few other manuscripts that were never published.

In *Reconciled*, I share my profoundly personal journey of healing and spiritual awakening after divorce and the challenges of co-parenting with my "wasband" (ex-husband). It told the story of how I transformed pain into a partnership built on mutual respect and collaboration. At the time, I dreamed of becoming a well-known author, helping women, couples, and families heal and grow. For over a decade, I devoted myself to spiritual counseling, coaching, and teaching stepcouples and moms how to navigate complex family dynamics and strengthen communication with their partners.

Almost ten years later, just days before my fifty-eighth birthday, I experienced a spiritual spark—a profound soul moment—in the shower, of all places. Inspiration often finds me there! I realized I had stopped dreaming and needed to reconnect with that part of myself. I asked my soul, *What am I supposed to do?* And then the answer came: write the second book.

My first book was for me—a profound healing journey—but I knew the second book was meant for them. *Who are they?* I asked. My soul responded: *The women.* At that moment, I understood my purpose with absolute clarity.

Spirit was unmistakably clear that *The Power of Inner Sparkle* would serve two purposes: first, to inspire readers by reminding women to let their light shine boldly. Second, to amplify the voices of women authors, empowering them to share their truths and fully embrace their inner light.

Throughout my life, I've been blessed to know countless women who radiate what I call *inner sparkle*. These women rise above fear and negativity, living authentically and aligned with their higher truths. They embody kindness, compassion, and warmth, inspiring others simply through their presence. Their inner sparkle holds the remarkable power to uplift, empower, and encourage those around them, illuminating a path for others to live more authentically. Perhaps you, too, know women like this.

This book celebrates every woman's inner sparkle. Each contributing author was chosen by divine design, and together, our stories weave a rich tapestry of resilience, strength, and transformation.

These pages contain the heartfelt stories of remarkable women who have triumphed over adversity, found the courage to embrace change, and trusted in their inner power. You'll witness their reflections on challenges and growth that inspire strength, wisdom, humility, forgiveness, gratitude, love, compassion, self-love, and an extraordinary sense of freedom.

Prepare to be inspired. Let these stories awaken your inner sparkle, reminding you of the light and love that reside within.

Together, we shine brighter.
Bobbi Wilcox
Creator and lead author of *The Power of Inner Sparkle*

Chapter 1

A WHISPER FROM WITHIN

"Go 'within' and listen.
The answers are always there, waiting to guide you."
And remember to "Throw that Sparkle Everywhere!"

By MaryJo Vaculin

In this heartwarming chapter titled "A Whisper From Within," MaryJo Vaculin takes readers on an emotional journey that begins with a young child's poignant experience of loneliness and fear while in the hospital. As she battles physical illness, her deep connection to her angels provides comfort and guidance, filling her with a sense of peace. Through vivid memories of her childhood, MaryJo shares her journey with celiac disease and the spiritual awakening that allowed her to find strength and resilience. Her story is a testament to the power of inner belief, divine guidance, and the love surrounding us.

MaryJo's ability to connect with her angels and trust in her inner wisdom has shaped her path, and in this chapter, she encourages readers to embrace their own light and share it with the world.

A WHISPER FROM WITHIN

I'm alone. Why am I all alone?

In the hospital bed, I glanced frantically to either side, hoping to see someone familiar. Shivers cascaded through me as my gaze drifted to the large window next to the bed where my parents had left me not long ago. Something was different about that window . . .

Its glass became a portal to another world beyond my reach, like a giant picture frame showing my five-year-old eyes are somewhere far away. Confusion raced alongside my heart. But then I saw them: Mommy and Daddy were through that portal, gracefully walking away from me, down a distant hall.

Panic bubbled in my chest, and desperation welled up inside of me. Why would they go away when I was sick? With a trembling hand, I pounded against the window and shouted, "Mommy! Daddy! Where are you going? Don't leave!"

I blinked as my eyes fluttered open, and suddenly I was 'really' awake. Everything came rushing back to me as the nightmare dissolved: the cold hospital room, the dim lights, the funny-smelling sheets, the lumpy mattress. Tears flowed softly, warming my cheeks as I curled into a small, scared ball, echoing the fear in my heart.

I shouldn't have sneaked that slice of bread down from the bread box in the kitchen. It didn't make sense why everyone else could enjoy the forbidden food and I couldn't. In my child's mind, I was pretty smart memorizing those creaks in the hardwood floor so I could tiptoe across it, pull the chair over, and whisk the treat back to my room. It was so yummy . . . but then my belly rumbled and screamed in pain.

Pulling the covers up on the hospital bed for comfort, I remembered how Mommy found me in the bathroom, tears streaming down my face. An asthma attack hit, too. My parents, loving and kind, rushed me to the hospital. Right then, I just missed them so hard it hurt.

With a little sniff, I took a brave look around the scary room. Quietly, I said a prayer to myself. I knew how much my parents loved me, and I knew they'd be back. A bit of strength grew, like a tiny light in the dark. My angels stayed by my side for the rest of the night, lighting up my whole room.

Mom and Dad returned the following day, and my heart was filled with peace. My mom's glamorous bouffant hairstyle was like a royal crown, with light brown hair and golden sparkles woven through it. Its sleek shape and sparkling highlights made it look magical. As my eyes followed her elegance to my dad, he stood tall with gorgeous dark hair slicked back, radiating his handsome charm. He was truly my buddy.

"Guess what, Mommy?" I began. "I saw you leave, going down the hall through the window."

"Sweetie?" Mom replied, glancing with an unsure smile at my dad.

I nodded with a grin, excited to share my whole angelic experience. "But it's okay because my angels stayed with me. It was beautiful! Everything shone brightly, and I could hear and feel them."

Mom and Dad exchanged beautiful smiles as they looked at each other, then at me. They held my hands and hugged me, saying, "We believe you; we understand."

Dad added, "Our family shares in these experiences, each with the special gifts given to us. Continue with your prayers and keep believing because God is with you, and your angels are always with you."

When we got home, I knew what was coming: I couldn't play outside even though the weather was beautiful.

The next day, early in the morning, Daddy helped me get ready for the day, giving me big hugs and kisses. He whispered, "Love you, Mouse," as he left.

In my room, I sat cross-legged on my bedroom floor, still not feeling very well, wishing things could be different.

"I'm worried about you getting sick again," Mommy told me empathetically. "And we don't want you to return to the hospital. You'll have to stay inside for now, sweetheart."

Sighing, lowering back strands of my long, blonde hair, I stared out of the two lovely windows of my room. One faced west, the other south, and sunshine poured in to bathe the hardwood floors in sparkling light. Why did it have to be such an extra beautiful day?

I liked the times when Mommy would tie knots on the back gate of our yard so I could at least be outside for a little while. By the time I worked all the knots loose, she had usually finished the laundry and could come up to be with me and have fun before I had to come back in.

I glanced at my dresser, toy chest, and bed, which was perfectly made, just like my gentle dad, the wonderful Marine, had taught me. Even though I gave in to being unable to go outdoors, I still approached one of the windows, loving the warmth of the sun on my skin. With a gentle push, I lifted the pane until it was fully open, embracing the crisp air as it danced past me. My bedroom was filled with the sweet fragrance of lilacs.

Our backyard had vibrant colors and scents that always greeted me when I opened my windows. Monarch butterflies fluttered past, heading straight for the flowering bushes to enjoy the nectar. A chorus of parakeets sang through the air in unique, cheerful chirps. I breathed in deeply, happily taking in the joyful concert. In the distance, the rumble of a train echoed from the hill. It was a familiar sound that wove itself into our daily lives.

Standing proudly in a semi-circle, all ten lilac bushes were heavy with delicate purple blossoms. I thought they were each a masterpiece, especially in the sunlight. The sweet aroma wrapped around me like a comforting embrace. Deep inside, I knew there was something more about this moment that was significant beyond the beauty of nature. The world outside was alive, telling me something, and a shimmering peace sparkled within me.

Settling down on the floor by my bed, I grabbed a few toys to keep me busy while Mommy was in the other room. I hummed to myself, content, and then something caught my eye. There was a mysterious glow forming on the wall opposite me. Curious, I peered at the enchanting light, guessing it was just some of the afternoon's sunshine. But when I looked closer, I saw something magical! There, on the plain, white wall, were children. Dozens of them waved at me with bright smiles.

I jumped to my feet and waved back.

"Hi!" I cried happily.

Their voices floated around me like the lilac-scented breeze, full of laughter and joy. But, just as quickly as they appeared, they faded away. Left behind was a sense of wonder. I sat back down, my heart racing. How could those kids be on my wall, beyond the beautiful trees, paths, and flowers? To have other children to play with, right here next to me, was like a dream come true.

Mommy said I had a weak immune system, which made it hard for me to be around big groups of real kids. I wished these angels could have stayed or that I could have gone back to their magical world to play with them.

Inside my sun-kissed bedroom, everything seemed to hum with possibilities. What if the glow returned and so did the children? What if I can step through the wall into their world? My heart filled with excitement, knowing I had to find out who those boys and girls on the wall were.

From then on, I sat on my comfy bedroom floor whenever I felt ill. The boys and girls on the wall would return to me, and I soon realized they were some of my angels.

Real kids (and many adults, too) didn't understand why I always got sick. My poor parents frantically watched me get sick over and over, no matter what I ate or drank. Nothing seemed to stay down, and my little body struggled to absorb nutrients, leaving me weak.

Finally, a curious and caring pediatrician sent my bloodwork to California for testing. That's when we had our crucial diagnosis: celiac disease. At the time, it was hardly heard of, although it had existed for centuries. My parents did everything they could to help set me on a course for a lifetime of dietary vigilance. But sometimes, little girls still had to sneak delicious pieces of bread.

My glowing angels would come back, appearing over and over. Their light sparkled in my room as if the wall opened into an enchanted world I saw through a child's eyes. Neither of us could go to the other side, but their existence in my realm helped me transcend the ordinary. I experienced their pure joy and innocence, so I wasn't all alone.

Because of them, a calming spirit embraced my soul. God's guiding light and love graced me because of these special little angels.

"We love being your angels, MaryJo," one of the shining little girls told me one day. "We're here to spend time with you and teach you."

I grinned back at her, blue eyes wide with curiosity. "What are you going to teach me?" I asked.

"How to go within," answered one of the boys, gesturing at his chest when he spoke. "So, one day, you can teach others how to do the same."

We told each other stories, and I reveled in the company that came with their enchanting light.

"You have a very special gift," they shared, "that you get to carry through life. You can listen, go within, and sometimes see."

Even when I was sick (often), I didn't mind being in my room because my spirit soared with the presence of my angels. At first, I didn't fully understand what everything they said meant; we just played and had fun times together. But as I grew older, these special children became my guides down the path of life. They taught me to listen carefully, trust my inner guidance, and that it would lead me in the right direction.

I still prayed a lot; a sacred refuge that connected me to God. As years went by, I also had the love of family and friends and the delicate guidance of those angels and companions who glowed with that divine light.

Eventually, I started to see that my disease was not a betrayal or a limitation but one of my most profound spiritual experiences. It was a sacred gift that taught me the art of going within. Amazingly, my parents always believed in my experiences and supported me no matter what. I was so blessed!

One day, when I was around eight years old, I was in my room playing with my angels. They looked at me, and one said, "You know that we love you, MaryJo."

"Of course," I replied, smiling. "Yes!"

They said, "We must go now."

My smile started to fade. "I don't understand . . ."

My angels looked at me and, in their bright light, said, "Do not be afraid. We are children's angels. Now that you are older, we will help other children now. You will always have your special angels with you."

After that, I never saw them again on my walls, no matter where I looked for them or how hard I searched. However, they did leave a lasting message in my heart: I can always go within and feel their presence along with my own angels.

As I got older, I explored celiac disease's 2,000-year history and learned about a key discovery during the 1940s by a Dutch pediatrician who linked wheat to symptoms during World War II. This research deepened and fueled my understanding of the disease's triggers and enduring impact. Celiac disease is a well-established and medically recognized autoimmune disorder. It occurs in genetically predisposed individuals when ingesting gluten protein found in wheat, barley, and rye. It triggers an immune response that damages the small intestine.

The damage can result in various symptoms and complications, such as digestive issues, malnutrition, and an increased risk of other immune disorders. The only effective treatment is adhering to a strict gluten-free diet, which enables intestinal healing and prevents further damage. My go-to meals include wholesome options like chicken, fish, rice, potatoes, fruits, and vegetables. I seldom dine out due to the risk of cross-contamination and tend to avoid most packaged foods available in stores today.

When I grew into a teenager and then an adult, it felt like my relationships with family and friends had transformed, matured, and evolved in the blink of an eye. This disease has been a constant in my life with no cure in sight, but I never give up on my research and advocacy.

When my two daughters were born, we faced the challenge of identifying their struggles with celiac disease, as well. As a single mother, it wasn't easy to navigate this journey at the time. However, our struggles only strengthened our bond as mother and daughters. I did my best every day to show them that my resilience could be an example for them to follow.

I have grown stronger, embracing every opportunity for adventure in my adult life. I have flown as the copilot in a few small planes, hang-glided, skated, fished, hiked, swam, waterskied, and traveled across the US and other countries. I have climbed mountains, attended exhilarating sports events, and even rounded up some cattle on horseback.

Life is too short not to dream big and play big.

I took this truth into my role as a mother, ensuring that my daughters and I have shared countless adventures, creating memories filled with joy and light. We ensure we have the right foods and know where the nearest bathroom is during our travels. Through our love, we stay connected to each others' well-being. These experiences have taught us the importance of supporting one another and cherishing every moment.

I became successful in my career journey as the co-owner of a prestigious technical institute. With this vision in mind, I laid the foundation of a company by assembling a team of trusted colleagues and friends. Together, we forged strong partnerships with industry giants like Microsoft, Novel, and Cisco, delivering cutting-edge technical training that set new standards in the field. I achieved significant professional milestones during my tenure and pursued my passion for motivational speaking and training. This dedication led me to develop innovative training courses and expertise with motivational insights.

Teaching adults became a dream come true. I helped them build strong connections and embrace their unique paths to fulfillment.

We discussed overcoming traumas, including how celiac disease affected me, like attending parties with limited gluten-free options or bringing in my own food to restaurants. It's tough, but I'm blessed with children, grandchildren, and friends who understand and support me.

One of the most rewarding experiences I had about five years ago was working with children and witnessing their growth. I had the honor of teaching struggling students how to read and served as an assistant director for drama productions. Words of validation became powerful tools, and hearing how I changed their lives confirmed that my guidance was exactly what they needed. I taught them that everyone faces unique challenges, like my own experience with celiac disease, and that these challenges don't define us.

If you look at me, I stand perfectly straight and proud. Yes, there is pain, but it doesn't rule or define me. I wake up daily thankful to be alive, ready to love and live.

I see the tapestry of my life as a journey woven with threads of resilience, love, and divine guidance. From the tender whispers of childhood dreams to the resolute steps of adulthood, each moment has been a stepping-stone leading me to the vibrant present I now cherish. The angels in my life—my two beautiful daughters and six radiant grandchildren—have been the beacons of light guiding me through the shadows of doubt and the storms of adversity. Their laughter and love have been my compass, steering me toward a life of purpose and fulfillment.

In the pages of my chapter in *The Power of Inner Sparkle*, I share the divine secrets that have illuminated my path, hoping to ignite the inner power within each reader. My journey, once marked by internal struggles and the weight of past health issues, experience, and growth to overcome it, has transformed into a testament of strength and a gift of inspiration.

Teaching others, especially adults, to believe in themselves has been both my mission and my healing. Now, I am thrilled to extend this passion to the younger generation through my children's book series. This new venture fills my heart with excitement and anticipation as I aim to inspire, educate, and empower children, nurturing their imaginations and guiding them toward a brighter future.

I stand at the threshold of new beginnings. I am filled with gratitude and anticipation for my life ahead. Through love, forgiveness, and genuine relationships, I have discovered that true success and wealth lie not in material possessions, but in this circle of authentic souls who walk beside us.

My intentions are set and my spirit is ablaze with the promise of creation and connection. Together with my family, I embrace the fullness of life, knowing that the greatest gift we can offer is ourselves unconditionally and with an open heart.

Let us walk together, cherishing each moment, and let our spirits glow with the joy of giving and gratitude. In doing so, we recreate the forgotten light within and share our luminous destiny with the world.

When my children were born, I began my day with a mantra: "Good morning, good morning, rise and shine," I say to my girls.

Recently, as I was blessed to be part of this women's group, I changed it slightly:

"Good morning, good morning, rise and shine. Throw that sparkle everywhere."

Now, that is how I start my day. It inspires my spirit with positivity and sets the tone for me to manifest my intentions. Gracefully, these words help me prepare for whatever the day will bring.

I know that our stories begin with the power within us. Despite all my challenges, I have learned to see the good in all things, trusting that God will take care of me and all of us.

All of your angels are closer than you think, on the other side of those windows, on the walls of your home, and in your heart. You are never alone.

I want to leave you with a special message:

> *May God's guiding light surround you; His Light is His Love. May all your angels hold their hands in a circle, wrapping around you with a comforting embrace, guiding you through this life.*

Always remember to throw that sparkle everywhere!
"I AM LIGHT"
By MaryJo Vaculin

MARYJO VACULIN BIOGRAPHY

MaryJo is a gifted, multifaceted motivational trainer, speaker, and author, passionate about guiding both adults and children on their journeys of personal growth, worthiness, self-care, and discovery of their voices. With years of experience in teaching and motivational training, she empowers individuals to unlock their inner greatness at home, in the workplace, and within their relationships. Her transformative classes and exercises help individuals build strong connections and embrace their unique paths to fulfillment

An accomplished photographer, artist, actor, and co-owner of a training company, MaryJo uses her creative talents to inspire and connect with others. Her volunteer work with the elderly and with SHEROES UNITED organization, One Billion Rising, and several different charity events reflects her deep commitment to community service. As a motivational trainer, she has shared her insights at various events, appeared on radio shows, and was featured on *Good Things Utah* and Oprah's Own Network with *SHEROES*. Her work has been recognized in publications like *HuffPost*, and she participated in the Parliament of the World's Religions, showcasing her dedication to fostering understanding and unity.

MaryJo is honored to contribute to *The Power of Inner Sparkle*, an inspiring compilation book created by women for women and the people who love them. She shares a chapter from her forthcoming Inspirational book, "The Secret Answers Within You," as well as a new children's book series that imparts valuable life lessons.

Her greatest love and joy come from her two beautiful daughters and six amazing grandchildren, who inspire her constant learning and growth.

CONNECT WITH MARYJO:

Follow on Social: IG & FB @maryjovaculinpalmer,
TT @maryjovaculin

CHAPTER 2

LIVIN' OUT LOUD:
TURNING SETBACKS INTO COMEBACKS

**"You are stronger than you know,
and your future is yours to create."**

By Andrea Cashdollar

In this deeply personal and transformative story, "Livin' Out Loud," Andrea Cashdollar invites readers into her journey of self-discovery, resilience, and redemption. With profound vulnerability, she shares the struggles of seeking external validation, the weight of unmet expectations, and the painful realizations that came with it. Through reflections on her childhood, her relationships, and the breakdowns that left her feeling lost and unseen, Andrea reveals how she began to embrace her true worth—not through accomplishments or approval, but through God's unconditional love.

She shows that it's not the external circumstances but the choices we make in the darkest of times that shape us into the women we are destined to be. This chapter is a moving testament to the beauty of reinvention, the unyielding power of self-love, and the courage to live out loud with purpose, no matter the obstacles.

LIVIN' OUT LOUD:
TURNING SETBACKS INTO COMEBACKS

Today, I stand at a crossroads—not one of uncertainty, but of clarity.

This is neither the beginning of my story nor the end, but the beautiful, messy middle where transformation unfolds. I am no longer who I once was, yet I am still becoming the woman God created me to be. For the first time, I am writing my own story—not as a passive observer but as the fearless author of my destiny, leaning on the Lord to guide my steps.

For too long, I lived for performance-based acceptance. Every achievement, milestone, and outward success was a desperate attempt to prove my worth—to myself, others, and a world that often felt indifferent. But the truth is that achievement without impact is empty. It is a shadow of fulfillment; an illusion that fades when the applause dies. I built castles of success on shifting sands, only to watch them crumble with the first gust of adversity. It was only when I turned to God and sought His purpose for my life that I began to understand that true worth is found not in worldly accolades but in His unconditional love and calling.

As a young woman, I dedicated two and a half years to completing a traditional four-year psychology degree at the University of

Northern Colorado, pushing myself to finish as quickly as possible. I believed that if I achieved this, I would finally prove my value to my mother and family—and, in turn, to myself.

I studied late nights and early mornings, and did whatever it took, sacrificing much, unconsciously convinced that this accomplishment would bring me the recognition I craved. Though I knew my mother loved me, we struggled to connect and truly see each other. More than anything, I longed for her absolute acceptance. I wanted to be seen and loved for who I was.

But when graduation day arrived, her response shattered the vision I had clung to for years. She barely acknowledged the milestone itself, offering only a passing remark: "It was a nice ceremony—now let's head home for the party."

In that moment, it became painfully clear: for her, this was never about my achievement. It was about her—the party, the guests, the appearance of pride. I don't think she meant to diminish my moment; in her own way, she was doing her best. But the validation I longed for—the recognition of my effort—was overshadowed by her need to celebrate in a way that made sense to her, leaving me feeling unseen and empty.

Without even realizing it, I had given away my power. I had allowed others to define my values, believing their opinions mattered more than my inner voice. I had let circumstances dictate my confidence, allowing the tides of life to toss me about like a rudderless ship. But in my brokenness, God was waiting. I was never truly alone. His hand had been guiding me, even in the moments I felt most lost.

LOST IN THE SEARCH FOR WORTHINESS

Even before the storms of adulthood hit, I carried a quiet burden. Growing up in the Midwest—born in Iowa, raised in Missouri, and moved to Colorado in high school—I often felt abandoned, isolated, and unworthy of love. I experienced a persistent sense of being alone and stranded from an early age, believing I was never good enough.

Everyone around me—my parents and much older half-siblings—had busy, fulfilling lives that seemed to swirl effortlessly around them, leaving little room for me. They had their own interests, hobbies, relationships, and activities, while I felt like the leftover; the in-the-way little kid. I wanted to fit in. I wanted to be seen for who I was. I wanted to be heard. I wanted to matter. I wanted my life to matter. I wanted to win. But mostly, I wanted to feel accepted and part of something. So, I became the good little girl who followed the rules, a master of masks, hiding my true self beneath layers of compliance and people-pleasing

Those feelings of emptiness and disconnection followed me into my teenage years and seeped into my adult relationships. I struggled with self-worth, sometimes feeling jealous of others' successes, oscillating between being overly dependent on those around me and pushing them away out of fear of rejection.

I wasn't always rooted in Christian values, and I didn't yet understand the connection between healing, faith, and love. But as I grew in my faith, I learned that true healing required more than just knowing about God's love—it required experiencing it. Even then, understanding the concept was different from living it. I knew Jesus loved me, but I didn't know how to love myself. My heart was like a garden overgrown with weeds of self-doubt, waiting to be tended with grace and self-compassion.

Over time, I built a life around external validation. I displayed every success as a trophy, hoping it would finally be enough to quiet the voice that told me I wasn't worthy. But the truth was, no amount of success could fill the void of self-doubt and insecurity.

I had become addicted to achievement, yet the more I accomplished, the emptier I felt. It was like chasing a mirage in the desert—always tantalizingly close but never, indeed, quenching my thirst.

Then, while I was still a college student, my father introduced me to the man who would become the love of my life. What were the chances of that? Little did I know that within just two short months, we would be engaged and, only months later, married—at just twenty-one years old. This whirlwind romance fast-tracked my feelings of worthiness. I started to feel good about myself, believing that being chosen was the ultimate validation.

We built a life together, a partnership that spanned eighteen years—a testament to youthful love and shared dreams. Yet, as the years passed, I regretfully acknowledge that I played a significant role in the decay of our marriage. I allowed my insecurities and my unresolved wounds to fester and erode the foundation we had built. I became so consumed with external validation and the pursuit of achievement that I neglected the emotional intimacy and connection vital to a lasting partnership. I lost myself in the roles of wife, mother, and entrepreneur, forgetting to nurture the woman I was at my core.

Those eighteen years, filled with the joy of raising our four children, buying and selling homes, and launching businesses, were also marked by a slow, insidious drift. I blame myself for not recognizing the subtle shifts and not addressing the growing distance between us. I allowed resentment to build, communication to falter, and our love to wither. It wasn't a sudden collapse but a gradual erosion; a quiet unraveling that left us both heartbroken.

Then, in the aftermath of my first divorce, I became a single parent to my four exceptional children and, later, my spirited daughter, Ady. Those early days were a maelstrom of emotions—regret for what could have been, loneliness whispering in the quiet hours of the night, and a depression that made even the simplest tasks feel insurmountable.

I remember sitting alone in my parents' home, feeling as though I had surrendered my power by allowing the failure of a union to define me. I was not prepared to be a single parent. I felt like a ship without a captain, tossed about by fear and uncertainty. The weight of responsibility was crushing, and the silence in the house after the children were asleep was deafening.

THE FIRE THAT FORGED ME

Faced with financial ruin, I watched helplessly as the security I had fought to build crumbled before me. Bankruptcy loomed, and I found myself lost, relying on food stamps just to scrape by. Depression, fear, and shame consumed me. In a desperate attempt to survive, I began cleaning homes—if I could clean just one house a day, I could make $100, enough to keep us afloat. That $100 meant a paid utility bill, gas for my car, or clothes for my young children. But as I scrubbed floors and wiped away other people's messes, I often found myself crying into dirty toilets, marinating in regret over my mistakes. No matter how hard I tried, I couldn't keep up.

The debts kept piling up, and the weight of it all was suffocating. Filing for bankruptcy felt like a shameful declaration to the world—a mark of failure, much like Hester Prynne's scarlet letter, branding me with the consequences of my mistakes. It was a humbling blow, much like the regret I still carry from my divorce from my first husband—another chapter of my life that felt like it had failed. But God was still writing my story. He was turning my trials into testimony, my pain into purpose.

The promise of a fresh start beckoned, and I was swept up in the hope of a second chance and remarried. For a fleeting moment, life granted me a reprieve—a chance to rewrite my story. Yet, the new marriage, filled with promises, very quickly crumbled under the weight of my past struggles and shame. Another divorce followed, leaving me drowning in regret.

I questioned every decision, tormented by thoughts of what might have been. The weight of regret, compounded by loneliness and deep depression, threatened to extinguish the spark that was desperately trying to ignite within me. I felt like a character in a tragedy, repeatedly falling victim to the same plot twists.

Yet, even as I wrestled with despair, a tiny seed of resilience grew, reminding me that even in the darkest times, there is room for renewal.

Just when I thought I had braced myself against life's blows, health challenges took hold, draining my energy and leaving me questioning whether I could ever rise from the ashes of my former life. In those moments, my early feelings of abandonment and unworthiness resurfaced, reminding me of my deepest vulnerabilities. Overwhelmed by the cascade of hardships, I sometimes considered surrendering to the darkness. It was as if God was testing my breaking point, pushing me to the edge of despair.

Tragedy continued to test my resolve. I lost both of my parents— my mom to cancer and later my dad to Alzheimer's—who had been my anchors in a stormy sea of emotions. Their passing left an emptiness that seemed impossible to fill. The world felt colder, the sky darker. I was adrift without my guiding stars.

Yet, amidst that despair, a tiny ember of determination began to glow. I realized that if I allowed my pain to paralyze me, my children and I would never have a future. So, I decided to risk everything and reclaim the power I had once given away.

I chose to become the architect of my own life, rebuilding from the rubble with unwavering resolve.

The messy middle of my story was where everything seemed to unravel. I faced the weight of past decisions, the sting of broken dreams, and the harsh reality that I had spent years building a life that looked good on the outside but felt empty inside. It was a dark night of the soul; a crucible where I was forged anew. But in those quiet moments, I could hear God's voice. He reminded me that I was not abandoned. "For I know the plans and thoughts that I have for you,' says the Lord, 'plans for peace and well-being and not for disaster, to give you a future and a hope." Jeremiah 29:11 (Amplified Bible)

Deep inside, a fierce desire to live out loud began to stir. I refused to let life's harsh lessons define me. I yearned to reclaim my identity—a woman who would never give up, keep dreaming despite the odds, and dare to risk it all for a better tomorrow. Slowly, I began to piece together the fragments of my shattered self, determined to create a new narrative that was as vibrant as it was unyielding.

I immersed myself in the things that had once brought me joy, rekindling my love for fashion and style as acts of self-expression. Every morning, as I dressed with care and creativity, I declared that I was more than the sum of my past mistakes and losses. It was my armor, my war paint, my proclamation of *self-love*.

CHOOSING A DAILY GRATITUDE PRACTICE

I've learned to transform my thinking, beliefs, and way of being by committing to daily practices that radically shift my mindset.

As one of my mentors always says, "Daily anything, changes everything."

My first daily practice is to write down ten things I'm grateful for—an act that reminds me of God's blessings even amidst chaos.

The second is to set three specific goals daily. Sometimes, long-term aspirations are written repeatedly until achieved, and other times, small, immediate objectives are what I focus on. This habit trains my mind to focus on progress, one deliberate step at a time.

Then comes the growth, daily growth. What am I reading, listening to, or choosing to submerge myself in to grow personally daily?

Most importantly, I choose to release my pain each day, giving grace to others, surrendering it to God, and transforming that pain into power. I now know that the life I build is not by my strength but through His grace.

I learned that what we focus on becomes our reality.

I no longer get the life I have by chance—I get the life I focus on. I control what I can control: my focus, the content I consume, and the people I surround myself with.

If the external world affects my inner state, I risk becoming a slave to it. So, I embrace the present and reject the addiction to my suffering—a home I once knew too well. Now, I focus on cultivating success, freedom, and love while being obsessed with the impact I can have on others.

I believe in serving, giving, and loving fiercely because the accurate measure of our lives is not in our excuses but in our faithfulness to the call God has placed on our hearts. He is the author of my story, and with Him, I am becoming the woman I was always meant to be.

We can build, be broken, and rebuild. I learned the power of working with mentors—people who have walked my path or are journeying toward where I want to go. I surround myself with people who get me, engaging with a trusted circle on online video meetings, either weekly or monthly, and meeting in person a few times a year. These communities fuel my growth and remind me that if others aren't winning, perhaps I need to share my successes more openly.

Look in the mirror—if you love who you are, you're like fine wine, only getting better with time. My success isn't just about personal gain, it's about increasing everyone's odds of winning.

THE REAL ESTATE REBEL: CREATING FREEDOM AND IMPACT

In my rebirth, I discovered a passion that would reshape my future: real estate. I am now the owner and CEO of The Cashdollar Group, which is brokered by eXp Realty, headquartered in the mountains of Colorado near Colorado Springs. I built my real estate company around the heart of transformation. We specialize in helping buyers, sellers, and investors accomplish their real estate goals while building a national real estate network.

I'm the founder and current president of Teller Housing Hub, a 501(c)(3) nonprofit organization that serves residents by bringing the community together, increasing homeownership, and connecting homeowners with trusted professionals.

Through these efforts, I organized a Colorado-based online women's real estate investing community—a space dedicated to empowering women to build wealth, transform their futures, and unlock new possibilities. What started as a simple idea has become a movement, proving that financial independence is attainable when we support and uplift one another.

As my journey evolved, so did my mission. I proudly adopted a new identity: The Real Estate Rebel. With this title came a deep commitment to helping women in real estate and entrepreneurs over forty build freedom-focused businesses. Within a supportive, like-minded community, we discover new ways to create financial freedom and design the lifestyle we've always dreamed of. We are aiming to win in every area of life—living out loud, finding unshakable confidence, and stepping into the best versions of ourselves.

We take bold action, using our God-given talents to create lasting impact and build residual income streams that lead to financial independence. And we do it while enjoying life—exploring new destinations, growing personally and professionally, and continually perfecting our craft. We're becoming the humans our results require, always striving to be our best in everything we do.

Yet, there was a time when fear held me captive—a fear of taking risks and of exposing myself to further heartache. The thought of putting myself out there, vulnerable and unguarded, was paralyzing. It was like standing on the edge of a cliff, knowing that the fall could hurt. Writing this chapter and sharing pieces of my journey felt like peeling back layers of my soul and offering them up for others to see.

The fear of judgment loomed large.

What if people disagreed with my story? What if my words were ridiculed, misunderstood, or dismissed? I thought.

The weight of those potential negative opinions kept me frozen, unsure whether to move forward or stay hidden in the safety of silence. I told myself I could say anything—but said nothing. It was easier to hide than to risk rejection or criticism.

But as I began to write, I realized that sharing my story—despite the risk—was the very thing that could set me free. So, I chose to step into the discomfort, trusting that the message, however imperfect, was worth sharing.

Through my healing process, I began to see risk differently. It wasn't something to avoid—it was the very thing that pushed me to live more fully. A defining moment came in 2022, when I boldly decided to leave an amazing top-tier real estate team I had been a part of since the beginning of my career. That environment had taught me so much, surrounding me with a team that set high standards and supported each other's growth. I'll forever be thankful for them.

Walking away from that safety net wasn't easy. The comfort of being part of a winning team with established systems and support was hard to let go of. But in my heart, I knew it was time to move on—to pursue something that aligned more deeply with who I was becoming. I chose to join a brokerage that reflected my evolving goals and vision, allowing me to grow and shape my business in a way that felt authentic and had no glass ceilings.

It was a risky move—one filled with uncertainty and the fear of leaving behind what was familiar. But taking that step forward in faith made all the difference. It proved that sometimes, you must step out of the familiar and into the unknown to find what's truly meant for you.

Over time, I reclaimed the power I had once surrendered. True strength comes from within, and the ability to shape our destiny lies in the choices we make each day. I embraced my scars as symbols of survival—each one a testament to battles fought and won.

LIVIN' OUT LOUD

Livin' Out Loud!

It's more than a motto—it's my business, my license plate, and the rallying cry of my journey. It is a declaration that life is meant to be lived boldly and authentically and with an unshakable inner sparkle.

I am redeemed! You set me free!—this is my heart's cry.

In the tapestry of my life, every thread—woven with early feelings of isolation, the heartbreak of unmet expectations, and the relentless pursuit of self-forgiveness through love, acceptance, and divine encounters—has come together to create a masterpiece that is uniquely mine. I've faced divorce, single parenthood, remarriage, blended family challenges, loss, financial hardship, and illness. Each trial tested me, yet I chose to rise through it all. I am proof that resilience, faith, and self-belief can turn pain into purpose.

I'm not who I used to be.

Faith, family, and the pursuit of purpose guide me forward. My greatest blessings are my five children, two bonus children, six grandchildren, and a devoted husband. And when I need a boost, nothing lifts my spirit like the pop, rock, R&B, and soulful hits of the '70s and '80s—the best eras ever for music!

This is my story, a testament to transformation and the limitless power within us all. To every woman reading this, know that:

Your past does not define you.

Your inner light is undeniable.

You are stronger than you know, and your future is yours to create.

Let's do this together. Let's live out loud, embrace our inner sparkle, and step into the life we were meant for.

"I AM REDEEMED."
By Andrea Cashdollar

ANDREA CASHDOLLAR BIOGRAPHY

Andrea Cashdollar, known as The Real Estate Rebel, is a trailblazing entrepreneur, Realtor®, and leader redefining real estate success. As the founder and CEO of The Cashdollar Group, she brings over twenty-five years of expertise in entrepreneurship, negotiation, sales, and business strategy. She empowers buyers, sellers, investors, and agents to navigate the market confidently.

Andrea has built a thriving career by creating powerful real estate communities and equipping professionals—especially women over forty—with the strategies, systems, and networks to scale their businesses. Passionate about financial, time, and location freedom, she helps agents design sustainable, multi-income-stream businesses while achieving a balanced, fulfilling life they love.

Andrea leads an international movement, guiding agents to break free from outdated industry models. Through strategic partnerships and a proven roadmap to freedom, she's building a global network of real estate professionals taking control of their futures—on their own terms.

CONNECT WITH ANDREA:

Email: andreacashdollar@gmail.com
Website: https://andreacashdollar.com/
Follow on Socials: IG @andrea_cashdollar, FB @andrea.booth. cashdollar,
LI @andrea-cashdollar
#RealEstateEntrepreneur #Realtor #Ceo #Founder #Author # Leader #RealEstateRebel

CHAPTER 3

THE BEAUTY IN CATASTROPHE

**"You are writing your own story—
just don't put down the pen."**

By Virginia Taft

In "The Beauty in Catastrophe,"Virginia Taft shares a powerful journey of love, loss, resilience, and redemption. What begins as a passionate romance unravels into heartbreak and abuse, the devastating loss of a child, and the courageous decision to break free from cycles of pain. As she navigates heartbreak, motherhood, and self-discovery, Virginia finds strength in the unlikeliest of places—within herself and in the love of two little girls in need of a home.

This is a story of the human spirit. It is a testament to the power of hope, the wisdom of listening to one's inner voice, and our ability to create our own life story.

* This chapter has Disclaimers 5 & 6

THE BEAUTY IN CATASTROPHE

My husband said, "People take kindness for weakness."
I did not realize he was talking about himself.

I had had previous relationships, but this one was special from the first night we met. Harold was intelligent, charming, and witty—and he chose me!

I appreciated Harold's humor, intensity, and passion. He described me as burning like an ember and himself as nitroglycerine.

Handle carefully—nitro explodes.

Harold's goal was to move to Idaho. Within a week, we were a couple. Two years later, we were married and on our way.

Harold was raised by his grandparents after his father deserted the family and his mother died. In addition to a broken family, he endured abuse and prejudice. My family struggled, but my parents were solid Midwesterners—strict but loving. My dad died at forty-nine, but I never thought of him as weak. Mom was compassionate and came from a long line of strong women who raised children in fatherless families. I came to appreciate their influence and belief that life is a learning experience; we can only control our response.

I believe people are basically good until they show me otherwise. However, the human spirit can be corrupted, especially by trauma and the lack of early nurturing.

Not all people are what they seem.

Before we were married, Harold just got angry. Things did not improve once we left the city where his French-Canadian and Hispanic origins were accepted. Harold did not fit into the predominantly white workforce of Southern Idaho. Although light-skinned, he was called "nigger" by the Mormon crew he started with. Ever the outsider, his income was inconsistent.

I worked at the Rehabilitation Institute of Chicago, but there were few such settings in Boise, so I started a private practice in occupational therapy. Harold mentioned that he did not recognize me at work, which I took as a compliment. At work, I was competent and in control.

I did not realize how much that threatened him.

Our savings purchased thirty acres in North Idaho, close to the Canadian border. We camped on our land, Harold found a few small jobs, and I traveled several hours each day to work. The challenges I thought we would face as a couple became a tinderbox. He graduated to throwing things.

With winter setting in, we moved to a decrepit little house in a town of 3,000. Harold was seldom employed, but I started working full-time for a child development center.

A cyclical pattern evolved. Harold became inert, unable to move, locked into depression. Then, he would exhibit frenetic energy. I tried to be understanding, to coax him out of it, but I grew frustrated and exhausted with the balancing act.

I noticed a pattern in myself. As he became angrier, I pulled myself into a shell of protection, not wanting to incur his wrath. Almost anything was an excuse to escalate—the dance of anger.

My mom was a consummate 1950s housewife. The home was her responsibility. Marriage was for better or worse. I assumed she would see me as weak, giving up, and not trying hard enough, which translated to not being good enough. When she learned of my trials, Mom was surprised.

"Why didn't you tell me? You don't need to be a doormat."

We purchased a dilapidated house that was somewhere between reconstruction and "you should have torn it down." Moving like rats from room to room, we rebuilt from foundation to roof. It is said that remodeling a house is a test of marriage. Despite having steadier work and a release for his energy, Harold's cycles became more extreme.

He began to destroy things. I stayed out of the way as much as possible. Suggestions were perceived as threats, and I became the target of his ire. A coworker who had been in an abusive relationship saw a bruise on my forearm. She mentioned it looked like someone had hit me. I made light of it.

"Just a bump on the arm. You know how it is when you're building. I bruise easily."

I felt both superior and defensive.

How dare you insinuate . . .

Embarrassment and shame washed over me.

She is right. It is okay to ask for help . . . and admit you need it.

When I mentioned it to Harold, I knew I was in trouble.

He belittled her, saying, "When you are hit with oranges in a sock, it hurts, but it doesn't leave bruises."

The warning was there.

Harold shared that his childhood emotional abuse was worse than physical abuse, yet he controlled me with taunts and degradation. I looked for help, but there were no women's shelters. I was sure I could handle it. The behaviors were insidious. A boundary was set, a line in the sand. He did not step over it, but when my attention was diverted, he put just a toe over and redrew the line.

"What happened?"

"How did it get this way?"

"What did I do wrong?"

Then, there was our baby.

MAY 18: MOUNT SAINT HELEN

The horizon looked black as Harold and I sped on our bikes toward town.

"Sure looks like some heavy weather coming in," he remarked.

Mount Saint Helens had erupted. By the time we reached home, ash had begun to fall. The radio let us know what had happened, but what to expect was unknown. The next morning, ash blanketed the town. The air was a thick, gray curtain—still and foreboding. Harold dropped me off at work and left before I found out the building was closed. I walked home in this otherworldly environment, not knowing if it could affect me.

After all, I am strong.

Little did I know I was pregnant. When we discovered the pregnancy, Harold played the proud papa but later admitted he was frightened. The combination of unemployment, as well as seasonal affective and bipolar disorders, created a potentially deadly mix.

I considered myself a strong and balanced person who faced most things calmly. However, my choice not to confront him and set firmer boundaries created a swamp of misery. I walked a tortuous tightrope. One wrong step and I was doomed. A plate thrown at the back of my head caused a headache and neck pain that my body still remembers.

It must be my fault. I can't do this without him . . . or can I?

JANUARY 5: BABY DAY

Our baby girl was born full-term but stillborn. Her heart and lungs never fully developed. It was attributed to "an arrested stage of development at six weeks gestation." That coincided with my walk home in the ash from Mount Saint Helens. It seemed surreal. I was devastated, hollow, and numb. Well-meaning people would say, "Oh, you'll have another child."

Little did they know.

Harold's rage seemed to dissipate. Maybe I was buried in my grief, gave in, or became less of a patsy. He seemed to have a handle on his emotions, talked about his early trauma, and appeared to have made peace with the demons of his past.

Childhood wounds resurface if not resolved.

Two years later, we were still unable to conceive. I thought we had turned a corner as we focused on this latest struggle. We went through degrading testing and fertilization treatment. I was okay with the two of us, but Harold knew how much I loved children. I had always wanted to have kids of my own and also adopt. He wanted to give some child the home he had never had.

We began looking at older kids or a sibling group. Each failed placement request felt like losing a baby all over again—a stabbing, gnawing pain in my hollow heart. It seemed hopeless.

Finally, I said, "We will look at three more. If they are unavailable, I'm done."

All three fell through.

The following week, our social worker called. "I think two little girls in southern Idaho would be right for you."

Tears streamed down my face as I looked at their sweet faces and read about the two sisters, ages five and seven. Although four girls were in the family, these two had been kept together through multiple placements.

They never lived for more than nine months in each place. Starting at birth, they passed from parents who dealt with drugs, alcohol, and mental illness to foster care. Finally, the State pressured the parents to relinquish their rights. The most recent foster family had started the adoption process and returned the children when the couple decided to divorce.

"They need us," Harold said simply.

We met them on a hot day in August and decided to travel to the zoo. Although they had only been there once, the oldest, Ava, stated proudly that she knew how to get there.

"You need us so we can show you the way," she stated.

I asked Kadie, who was five, what she liked to do.

"Anything Ava likes to do!"

Both responses were prophetic.

The girls arrived for a six-month pre-adoption placement just in time for school to start. It seemed the sun had broken through.

A family at last!

I worked full-time with various agencies and traveled several hours each day but had flexibility with a fantastic after-school day-care. Work and caring for the girls was more than enough for me to handle, but Harold expected me to help buy and run a real estate business. His moods darkened with the weight of these new responsibilities. He became short-tempered with the girls, taking perverse pride in making Kadie cry over imagined disobedience.

Strike one. I would not let these children be abused.

I decided to surprise him for his birthday and visit our friends in Canada. Harold seemed excited at first. I packed everything into the car and prepared the girls to leave the following day. Once they were in bed, I talked excitedly about the trip. He decided he was not going. This was not a new tactic. There had been other times when plans were made and he would back out at the last minute, but I thought we had moved past that foolishness.

"I did all this to surprise you; everything is ready to go. This is our first time traveling as a family, and our friends are excited to see the girls."

He was adamant. "I won't go."

"I am going. I would love for you to come too, but if you insist on staying home, we are going anyway."

"Go ahead then!"

I descended the stairs ahead of the deluge, with my clothes thrown after me. The girls stood in their doorway, wide-eyed and frightened.

"What's happening?"

Strike two. The kids didn't need this. They had been through enough already. I could leave—they couldn't.

With as much calm as I could muster, I replied, "We are just going to leave a bit earlier. You can sleep on the way."

Our friends greeted the girls warmly but were not surprised that Harold had not come. Their support helped me to gain perspective. The girls needed to return to school, and I needed to work. I had to decide.

Now what? Should I stay in a motel until we could move out?

I finally called Harold, who apologized profusely and asked us to come home. I agreed that I would if he would go to counseling with me and clean up before we got home. He agreed, cleaned up, and was contrite for a few tense weeks.

Mom visited for Christmas, and we put on a game face. However, when I looked at the photographs, I saw Ava's worried expression, her arms reaching out between us, trying to hold us all together.

Harold agreed to go to counseling, but I began to look into apartments . . . just in case . . .

We were in the kitchen. Harold began sorting dry beans and the girls were seated at the table. Something triggered him and he flung beans all over the kitchen and stormed out. We were puzzled. I felt that slow burning ember flame into anger.

"Mom, are we going to clean it up?" Kadie asked.

"Yes," I replied.

. . . and this was the last time. Strike three, We were out!

Any remaining illusions I had about saving my marriage were shattered. The discomfort of where you are has to be more than the fear of moving forward.

We left, taking only clothes and sleeping bags. Harold went to counseling once but described the interaction with foul words. After all, he had no problems. The relationship was dead, despite his pleading.

"You made it too easy," he said. "I knew if I did not want to do something, you would take care of it."

He was right. If something needed to be done, I just did it. In that process, I may have emasculated him and made him the child, and he chose to act the part.

Harold's sister called me to ask if we were okay because he was "hearing people" in the empty house. He told me how I was a bad parent for letting the girls walk to school because "someone might take them."

Was that someone him?

My friend had been in a similar situation.

"People think you can just walk away. It isn't that easy. If he threatens to hurt or kill you or the kids, you have to take it seriously," she cautioned me.

When the social worker came to visit, I explained the situation.

"Do you want to keep the girls?" she asked.

There was no question in my mind, no hesitation. "They are my children; I will fight for them if needed."

"At age five and seven, they are considered unadoptable. Look what they have been through," she said. "You supported them all this time, so I see no reason to move them if you want to adopt them as a single parent. Let's see what the girls have to say. I notice Ava keeps coming into the house and looks very serious."

The social worker asked if Ava wanted to have me as her forever mom. Ava snuggled into my lap and gazed up at me.

"I can imagine I am your baby," she said.

Kadie came in next.

"Do you want Ginny to be your forever mom?" the social worker asked.

"Sure, but can I go home with you for today?" Kadie replied.

We laughed. Kadie looked puzzled, oblivious to the gravity of the situation.

I filed for divorce and custody of the girls, and purchased a car on the same day. Although left with mountainous debt, I breathed a sigh of relief. Finally, some rain had nourished me when I felt like a dry leaf in the desert.

MAY 18: ANOTHER BIRTH

Eight years after Mount Saint Helens erupted, we celebrated Adoption Day. The girls rode their new bikes in the neighborhood by the house I had just purchased. Mom summed it up: "You were meant to be together. It just took you a long time to find each other."

Kindness does not mean weakness. You have inner strength. Give yourself permission to be loved.

The journey to the 'birthing' of my adopted children gave me insights that I used as a single parent of two traumatized children. Often, we look for a great revelation; a dramatic moment when everything comes into focus. For me, it was more "Hmmmm, what is this about?" than a great "AHA!"

I follow the Zen proverb, "Even after enlightenment, you still have to do the laundry."

I can respond if I listen to that still, quiet voice of inner knowing. A rough and ugly stone can hold a beautiful jewel if I only look inside. Little nuggets of wisdom gleaned from experiences draw me along the path.

When something feels right—or doesn't—I make a choice.

My oldest daughter told me she dreamed she fell off a bridge into the water, and Harold just walked away. It took years for her to understand that leaving was best for all of us.

"I cannot change what happened to you. I can only show you that I love you, that you are valuable, and that you don't have to hurt people when you are angry. My wish for you is to be all that you can be, and I will do all I can to help you get there," I told them.

How do you parent traumatized children who were not parented but abused and neglected? They needed constant assurance that I was not leaving, that I was stable.

Two pairs of eyes watched me intently as I reached for the beer I ordered with my pizza.

"No, girls, I am not going to get drunk and crazy," I shared with them.

Both visibly relaxed. We talked about how alcohol affects people and how they might face challenges.

They displayed funny, cute, and sweet things like dressing the cat as baby Jesus or bringing me lilacs after my hysterectomy. However, they seemed drawn to danger: leaving the house in the middle of the night in a thunderstorm, setting fire to Christmas decorations, and stealing to fill the emptiness. I learned to listen to that little voice when something seemed 'off' to get above the level of the problem. I was constantly on high alert.

Thankfully, I had support from my mother and friends, who helped out but did not judge. My work, at times, was a refuge. Life was a roller coaster, and we were hanging on for dear life.

I have often said I am all religions, but none. I take from each of the parts that speak to me. Religion is a way to practice your spirituality, but your spirituality is your own. We joined a Unity church after trying several others. There, I felt love, acceptance, and support for single parents. My daughters liked it because "We can understand it."

Mom and I viewed a documentary called *Children of Rage*. We looked at each other when it ended and knew it could have been written about my girls.

When Ava started running away at age ten, life became darker. Soon Kadie followed the pattern.

"No, it is not okay to throw the cat against the garage, abuse your sister, stow a knife under your mattress, or beat up your grandmother."

I returned home one night to find Mom and Kadie locked in the bedroom. Ava was roaming the house, threatening them. We needed help.

Ava was admitted for psychiatric assessment, and more early trauma surfaced. I looked at their adoption day photo, screaming and crying. "How could you do this to your children?"

Because this was done to their parents, and we must break the cycle.

We tried counseling, but my kids could out-counsel every counselor except for one. He helped Mom, and I understand that kids who are nurtured early are like grapes; juicy and full of life. Those not nurtured are like raisins; they may be challenging, sweet, and survivors, but you cannot make them into a grape by just loving them enough. It is like trying to fill an empty well with no bottom.

I agreed, except I do not believe any love is ever lost.

He said they would not get it in their teens or twenties, maybe in their thirties or forties, maybe never. "It" means that you have responsibility for your own life. It is not all about what other people have done to you.

Both girls were placed out of the home by age of thirteen. I knew they needed more than I could provide. Through multiple placements, I never gave up on them and kept in contact as much as possible. For many years, I was considered the enemy, which was deeply painful. They gradually let go of their anger towards me and are recovering now. It is a lifelong process for all of us. Two of the best days of my life were when my youngest called one day.

"Mom, I am tired of being angry over things that happened when I was thirteen, and I want to be your friend."

And later the oldest called to say, "I want my life back. I choose to live."

The counselor asked me, "Why did you adopt these children? No, not because you wanted kids and a family. If you discover that seed, there is strength in that you can draw from."

As we headed home that day, Mom asked me if I had figured it out. I looked across the valley at the scattered dark clouds contrasted against the intense blue October sky.

"Isn't it dramatic?"

Mom looked at me. "Is that it?"

I thought a moment. Then I knew. "I love a good challenge."

We both laughed.

". . . and I want to make a difference."

Did I rescue them, or did they rescue me? We rescued each other.

Until today becomes tomorrow, we cannot see the beauty in catastrophe

I can write my own story. I don't want to put down the pen—not just yet.

"I AM UNLIMITED."

By Virginia Taft

VIRGINIA TAFT BIOGRAPHY

Virginia Taft, OTR, occupational therapist and myofascial release practitioner, is drawn to the mind-body connection, practical spirituality, and empowering women. As a business owner for over forty years, she has taught nationally and internationally.

Her published works are related to health care, business, inspirational, and motivational topics. Virginia continues to expand her work as an author, seeks new experiences, and especially enjoys travelling to third world countries. She supports "Together Women Rise," an international community of women dedicated to global gender equality, as well as Family Promise, which supports homeless families.

Virginia's book, *The Memory Box Journey*, is a memoir, travelogue, and guide to help others share their stories. Upcoming books in the series include: *A Little Bit of Blue*, dedicated to caregivers, and *A Bouquet of Seasons—Reflections on Life*. Virginia is available for speaking engagements, media interviews, and provides workshops.

"I am honored to be a co-author in *The Power of Inner Sparkle* by Bobbi Wilcox. Both to share my journey of adopting two traumatized children as a single parent, and also to connect with other women who have discovered their Inner Sparkle."

Life goes best when we listen to that still, small voice within.

CONNECT WITH VIRGINIA:

Email: taftve52@gmail.com
Website: www.virginiataft.com
Social media: IG & FB @virginiataft.choicevoice2u
#author #speaker #therapist #voiceoveractor

CHAPTER 4

FROM DEATH'S DOOR TO LIFE'S CALLING: A JOURNEY TO HEALING AND PURPOSE

"Nobody can love you as much as you love yourself."

By Katy Rose

In "From Death's Door to Life's Calling: A Journey to Healing and Purpose," author Katy Rose takes readers on a courageous and transformative journey from the brink of death to the discovery of her true purpose. This deeply personal chapter invites us into her world, where years of emotional trauma, toxic relationships, and a broken body led her to a pivotal moment—facing the choice between life and death.

Katy's story is one of resilience and self-discovery, where a quiet surrender to death became the catalyst for her miraculous recovery. This chapter is a warm invitation for anyone feeling trapped by their past or overwhelmed by their circumstances to find hope, embrace their inner strength, and rediscover their true self. Katy Rose's message is clear: healing is possible when we choose to listen to our bodies, honor our emotions, and embrace the power of self-care and love.

FROM DEATH'S DOOR TO LIFE'S CALLING: A JOURNEY TO HEALING AND PURPOSE

I f I had kept treating my body the way I had been, I wouldn't be here today. What was unfolding before me was a choice—life or death. And I knew, without a doubt, that I was dying.

I lay in bed, too weak to move, the weight of the blankets pressing down on me like an unbearable burden. Even if I had wanted to call for help, my voice was too faint, swallowed by the silence. I could feel myself slipping away, surrendering to the darkness.

A calm knowing washed over me—I understood that, with my agreement, I could let go, surrender to death, and pass to the other side. I was frail and drained. I had fought for so long and had nothing left to give. There was no fear, no desperation, only a quiet certainty, like the stillness after a long storm. I felt it in the way my breath slowed and in the strange lightness that wrapped around me. The struggle was over. For the first time in years, I wasn't reaching for healing or hoping for more—just resting in the certainty that the fight had ended.

And so, I succumbed and agreed—it was time for me to die.

The year was 2015. I was forty years old, living in beautiful, sunny San Diego, California. I had been out of work for six months due to my illness. My marriage was toxic. I had lost all hope.

Looking back, I saw the pattern. I had been trapped in three dysfunctional marriages—each one filled with minimizing, limiting, and toxic cycles. I married for the first time at eighteen to escape a dysfunctional childhood, then divorced, only to enter another marriage a few years later. And then another. Each relationship was a continuation of my disease, repeating the same patterns of narcissism, judgment, criticism, and control. Each one kept me caged.

But no moment in my life was darker than that day, lying on what I believed to be my deathbed.

BRACELETS, BEAUTY, AND THE BRINK OF DEATH

I felt a presence as I gave way, fading into the darkness. My friend's spirit—who had died years earlier—came to me. During our seventeen-year friendship, we shared deep intimacy and sisterhood. She had always needed to keep her hands busy—crafting, creating. She was constantly making bracelets, stringing together beautiful chains and beads. I had wads of her bracelets in my jewelry box.

I wasn't someone who wore much jewelry. I used to laugh and say, "Heidi, what will I do with all these bracelets?"

She would grin and sway, "I don't know—add them to your collection."

She had passed far too soon, taken by tragedy. But at that moment, as she came to me in spirit, I knew she was trying to tell me something.

I tried to shift my body in bed, struggling to move just enough to see my wrist—where I had once worn her bracelets. But it was bare. I remembered the bracelets in my jewelry box. Weakly, I brought my wrist closer to my heart, trying to imagine them there, longing for one last moment of beauty before my spirit slipped away.

I needed beauty.

I had gone from stepping into the darkness to craving beauty . . . desperately. Somehow, I managed to twist my arm slightly, and at that angle, it struck me as unexpectedly beautiful. The longing became overwhelming. I *needed* those bracelets on my wrist.

With what little strength I had left, I crawled to my jewelry box, pulling myself inch by inch across the floor. I loaded my arm with as many bracelets as I could. Looking back now, I don't know how I managed it—how I found the strength to move, let alone put them all on. But I did. Then, just as weakly, I crawled back to bed, my arm heavy with the weight of her love.

I wore those bracelets for six months.

In that fleeting moment, something shifted. A desire sparked inside me. A desire to live. A desire to embrace beauty. A desire to see myself whole again.

HOW EMOTIONAL TRAUMA AND FOOD BECAME MY COPING MECHANISM

Growing up in rural Oklahoma in the woods, home life was extremely stressful. At a young age, I was sexually abused, which led to compulsive eating. Whenever food was put in front of me, I always wanted second and third portions as a way to cope with my emotional trauma. When I was in second grade, I had some baby fat, and my mom became obsessed with it, putting me on a diet. I did strange things as a child; actions that would later lead to extreme health issues in adulthood. For instance, I brushed my teeth with bleach and took inappropriate amounts of antibiotics. I even took diet pills—all of which would contribute to a poor gut microbiome in my adult life.

I grew up with bulimia, an eating disorder, and I always thought I was fat. It wasn't until my forties, while looking at a childhood picture, that I realized I wasn't actually fat; I had body dysmorphia, a mental condition that distorted my perception of my physical appearance.

During my early twenties to thirties, I ballooned to 240 pounds on a 5'6" frame. I struggled to fit into airplane and theater seats and stopped buying clothes in size twenty. I ate four bread baskets at an Italian restaurant before the main course came. Despite my best efforts to stop compulsively eating, I couldn't. I had so much PTSD around going to bed hungry that I couldn't stop eating before bed.

During this period, my mental and physical health were spiraling. I was on a long list of psychiatric medications and was mentally dysregulated to the point that I couldn't keep a job. Mentally, I was not stable.

Then, I discovered Dr. Daniel Amen, a functional psychologist and the foremost leader in brain scan technology. His studies showed the impact that different foods have on brain chemistry. While I had succumbed to the idea that I would always be obese and that I could never overcome it, I desperately wanted my brain to work the way other people's brains worked.

Through learning from Dr. Amen, I slowly began to integrate his recommendations. For example, I switched my bedtime snack from carbohydrates to protein, and I immediately noticed changes in my brain health. Over the course of a year, by taking one step at a time, I was able to get off all psychiatric medications and, as a byproduct of my efforts, actually lost ninety pounds.

While losing weight wasn't my primary focus, it happened naturally due to the small changes I made in my eating. As time passed, I began working out, eating healthier than anyone I knew, and experiencing significant improvements in my mental health. I could hold down jobs, but my stomach health, energy, and fatigue were still challenging to manage.

After taking antibiotics for a sinus infection, my health took a dramatic turn, and after six months, everything came to a head, and I lay on my deathbed.

BREAKING FREE: HOW FUNCTIONAL MEDICINE RESTORED MY LIFE

Things were fuzzy during those six months. But after the day with the bracelets—after experiencing my friend's presence—something shifted. I found myself in a functional medicine doctor's office.

A longtime friend had reached out to me. Her husband, once a chiropractor, had gone to the Institute of Functional Medicine and become a functional medicine practitioner. He had grown tired of seeing so much illness in the world and wanted to do something different. When she discovered what was happening to me, she said, "Katy, you need Jason to work on you."

I stared at her blankly. "I don't even know what you're talking about."

"He's done all of this," she insisted.

It had been years since I had seen either of them, but I had nothing to lose. I had no money and was on disability. Everything in my life was crumbling. But when I walked into his office, Jason didn't hesitate.

"We've got to get you well," he said. "Don't worry about the money. We'll figure it out. Let's start with some tests."

He ran more tests than any doctor had ever run on me—more tests than I knew were possible. When the results came back, everything finally made sense.

"If you feel like you've been dying, it's because you have been," he said.

I had nine bacterial overgrowths in my digestive tract, four of which had gone pathogenic. I was suffering from severe hyperthyroidism and full-blown liver failure. I had been on death's doorstep.

I wept as they held me. I could barely sit up in the chair as I absorbed the news. I felt like a hollow, empty shell. But then Jason looked me in the eyes.

"We're going to get you well."

They put me on an intensive elimination diet. That wasn't hard because, at that point, I wasn't eating anyway. My life had been reduced to a cycle of sleep and survival.

When I woke up, I drank chicken broth. After having four major bowel blockages that year, even the smallest spoonful of solid food would make me throw it up. My digestive tract had shut down completely. I couldn't process food. I would lie on the floor, trying to give myself an enema. Then I'd crawl to the toilet, trying to release anything. But nothing came out except water.

It was weeks and weeks of the same cycle: sleep, sleep, sleep, wake up, broth, enema, crawl to the toilet, crawl back to bed, repeat. It was insane.

Jason gave me copious amounts of herbs, nutraceuticals, and supplements. Six weeks later, something miraculous happened. I was in the kitchen, making breakfast, and singing.

I WAS BACK!

It took years to repair my body entirely, but the light was returning at that moment. I was alive. I still needed copious naps for the next three years, but I was finally healing.

During that journey, I became obsessed with functional medicine. I kept asking myself, *What went wrong in my body?*

What had damaged me physically?

What had damaged me emotionally?

What role had I played in my own illness?

What had I been taught that led me to harm myself unknowingly?

And then, more questions arose.

What is it that makes the body repair itself?

What was I doing that got in the way?
Why couldn't the medical system help me?
Why are doctors failing people like me?

I dove into what I call my personal PhD program—because learning about functional medicine became as essential to me as breathing. I devoured everything I could, trying to understand the body, healing, and the flaws in our medical system.

And then, I came out the other side.

People who had watched my journey were stunned. "What gives? You were obese and inarticulate, then you were emaciated and dying, and now you're shouting from the rooftops about functional medicine."

I couldn't stop talking about it. I had to share what I had learned. And so, almost without realizing it, a practice began. I started backfilling my knowledge with certifications and formal training.

But amid all that learning, I continued to work on my recovery and my body, and I had an epiphany:

Nobody can love me as much as I love myself.

And that realization—born from my healing—changed everything.

TRAUMA BECOMES MY WISDOM AND MY JOY

Most people understand what past trauma is, but not everyone knows the glory of recovery. Whether it's a toxic marriage, difficult parents, or a betrayal by a sibling, everyone has their version of trauma. I often think of mine as a journey—one that keeps circling back to me.

Self-sacrifice. Self-denial. Self-dismissal. These were the patterns I lived by, whether poisoning myself with excessive amounts of food or numbing my emotional pain in unhealthy ways. It all stemmed from one core issue: I wasn't coping with my trauma. I wasn't allowing myself to feel my feelings.

Many experiences from my past—both in childhood and adulthood—felt dirty and messy, like wading through thick, suffocating mud. I picture it like this: a rundown shack with a decrepit wooden porch. Beneath that porch, pressed against the house, is a dark, filthy space. That's where I was—trapped in my trauma, unaware of just how deep I was in it. Desperately, I searched for a way out, clawing for freedom.

The darkness was overwhelming, but as I turned to look for a way forward, I spotted a glimmer of light. To reach it, I had to push through the heaviness, crawling toward that light even when I felt weary, alone, and afraid. Yet, somehow, I summoned the courage and inner strength to keep moving through the muck.

Eventually, I broke free. I got out from under the mess. Some people escape their trauma and never look back, refusing to deal with it again. But I didn't want to run. I wanted to face it.

So, I stood up. I wiped myself off. I put my hands on my hips, looked back at that dark place where I had been stuck for so long, and said, *You had me down, but I am brilliant and amazing! And I am free!*

Trauma does not define me. I stand tall on that porch, hands on my hips, and I make it my platform. From here, I can teach others that they can rise above. They can stand proudly on what once held them down. I celebrate my survival. I embrace my freedom.

This is the moment when trauma becomes wisdom. And from wisdom, trauma transforms into joy. It's a sweet, sacred shift.

My friend Havilah and I often talk about this. She says, "Those who have trudged through the muck and climbed to the top of it see life differently. Every little thing sparkles more because of what they've endured. Once you've faced the darkness, the light shines brighter. The contrast makes it even more beautiful."

THE MOST IMPORTANT RELATIONSHIP: ME

I now believe that healing from trauma requires deep self-attention. I had to put the brakes on all other relationships and turn inward, fully committing to self-love. Only then did my relationship with myself begin to shift. It was in this sacred space that self-love became my foundation.

The most important relationship I needed to nurture was the one I had with myself. I had to accept myself, see my own beauty, and recognize my own worth. The lack of self-love, self-respect, and self-nurturing had led me to the brink of destruction. I now see that my disconnection from myself was the root of so much of my suffering. In suppressing my emotions and burying my true self, I lost years to self-loathing and struggle. But in embracing my authenticity, I have found healing, self-love, and inner peace.

Through this process, I have learned to practice self-nurturing and self-love. I now lean into my preferences, trust my inner wisdom, and embrace the power of my inner sparkle. I listen to the guidance of my higher power—God, Source, or whatever you choose to call it. To me, it all feels the same.

At this stage of my life, I've come to a profound realization: *My job is to love myself.*

I honor the precious jewel that I am. And in doing so, I am never truly alone.

Today, I am in a deep and meaningful marriage with my husband, a man I adore. Everything else fell into place because I learned how to love myself first. He is my best friend, my rock, my safe space. I can lean on him for anything. He lifts me up, soothes my wounds, and brightens my world.

I am so incredibly grateful for him. Our twenty-year friendship has evolved into the most magical love and partnership I have ever known. And it all began with learning to love myself.

My Functional Medicine Practice: A Holistic Approach to Healing

Outside of my love for myself and my wonderful husband, nothing fills my heart more than the work I get to do every day. So often, the people I serve are just like me—turned away by doctors who couldn't figure out what was wrong, dismissed, or even gaslighted into believing nothing was amiss. The truth is that our medical system is broken; it rarely looks deep enough. I often say it's easier to hook a car to diagnostics than to assess a human properly!

Many people suffer from physical manifestations not only of the toxic environment we live in but also of the deep mental and emotional wounds stored in the body. Healing requires more than treating symptoms—it requires uncovering the root causes that go far beyond what traditional medicine tends to explore.

I like to give people the analogy of being born with a small bucket in their hand, labeled "toxicity." At birth, that bucket is empty or nearly so. But as we go through life, we steadily fill it with toxins. When the bucket overflows, we experience symptoms—the visible signs of accumulated toxicity spilling over into our bodies.

What's even more fascinating is how emotional trauma and stress act like a wedge beneath the bucket, tilting it and causing it to spill even faster. People go through life unknowingly 'sloshing their toxins' everywhere, without ever stopping to examine what's filling their bucket so quickly—or how they might remove the wedge of trauma and stress to slow the overflow.

This ties directly to the denial of self I talked about earlier. What's truly surprising is that women are struggling the most. Consider this: it is now widely recognized that throat and thyroid health issues are often linked to not speaking your truth—to the act of suppressing emotions.

When we silence ourselves, we don't just carry the weight emotionally; our bodies bear the burden, too.

This is the work I love—the work God has blessed me to do. Through intensive lab testing, we can identify the external toxins filling the bucket, and through deep, heart-centered connection, we can uncover the traumas and stress that cause it to spill over even faster.

Without this kind of holistic approach, true healing remains out of reach. We *all* need this work to get *truly* well.

One of my favorite examples is a sweet client of mine, only in her sixties, whose body was riddled with pain from rheumatoid arthritis and fibromyalgia. She was on extensive medications—not just for pain but also for high blood pressure, hypothyroidism, and high cholesterol. Even the simplest tasks had become a struggle. She couldn't walk from her door to her car without a cane or complete a load of dishes without stopping to rest. Every movement was a challenge.

Together, we worked to uncover the toxins filling her bucket and the stresses tipping it over. She was committed—she did the work! I always remind my clients that they are the CEO of their own health, while I serve as their dedicated research assistant. I can provide the best guidance, but ultimately, the responsibility lies with them. And she rose to the challenge. She diligently worked to remove toxins, both externally and internally, while also transforming her relationship with stress.

Within six months, she was off pain medication and walking on the beach with her family on vacation. Yes, you heard that right—walking on the beach! Within a year, her doctors took her off *all* her other medications because she no longer needed them. In her mid-sixties, she didn't just regain her health—she reversed her biological age and reclaimed years of her life. And now, these won't just be extra years; they will be *good* years because she's no longer just surviving—she's thriving.

In many of his talks and books, Wayne Dyer used to say, "When you change the way you look at things, the things you look at change."

Healing begins the moment we shift our perspective on food, health, and ourselves. We reclaim our inner sparkle when we stop fighting our bodies and instead listen to them. As we heal, that transformation ripples outward because we are all connected.

If you're ready to break free from the cycles of imbalance, emotional eating, and disconnection from your body, I invite you to step into a new relationship with your health. Are you ready to reclaim your health and step into your inner sparkle?

Let's take the first step together, unlocking a life of vibrant well-being, true connection, and lasting transformation.

"I AM BEAUTY"
By Katy Rose

KATY ROSE BIOGRAPHY

Katy Rose is a certified functional medicine health coach, diagnostic nutritionist, and functional genomics practitioner with a heart-centered and intimate practice. At fifty years old, she brings both deep expertise and a compassionate approach to guiding her clients toward optimal well-being. Originally from Northeastern Oklahoma, Katy now resides in San Diego with her husband, where she continues her nationwide mission of helping individuals reclaim their health.

With a keen focus on identifying and addressing the root causes of health concerns, Katy takes a personalized, holistic approach to healing. She integrates gut health, hormone balance, metabolic function, nervous system regulation, and lifestyle factors to create tailored wellness plans that restore balance and vitality. Understanding that true healing goes beyond symptom management, she empowers her clients with the tools and knowledge they need to thrive.

Through her work, Katy provides a supportive space where clients feel heard, understood, and empowered to take charge of their health. Her passion lies in helping others navigate their unique health journeys with grace, science-backed strategies, and an unwavering commitment to whole-body wellness.

For more information about Katy and her functional medicine practice:

Email: katy@katyrose-coaching.com
Website: www.KatyRose-Coaching.com
Follow on Socials: IG @KatyRoseEffect

THE CONNECTION CODE: UNLOCKING THE SECRETS OF MEANINGFUL RELATIONSHIPS AND PERSONAL GROWTH

"When we take the time to truly understand and connect with ourselves, we create a solid foundation for personal growth and emotional well-being."

By Lacey Nelson

In this deeply moving chapter, Lacey Nelson takes us on a courageous journey through the pain of her past, sharing how the process of healing begins with self-awareness and vulnerability. With raw honesty, she recounts the trauma of her early childhood and the emotional walls she built to protect herself from the pain. Lacey reveals how, in the pursuit of moving forward, she unknowingly disconnected from herself—and the profound impact that disconnection had on her relationships and

* This chapter has Disclaimers 4 & 5

well-being. Through confronting her wounds, she discovers that true strength lies not in hiding our pain but in embracing it.

Lacey's story offers hope, showing that no matter how deep the hurt, healing and meaningful connections are always within reach.

THE CONNECTION CODE: UNLOCKING THE SECRETS OF MEANINGFUL RELATIONSHIPS AND PERSONAL GROWTH

Personal growth begins with self-awareness. We must understand what drives us and recognize how our upbringing has shaped where we are today. Often, the most difficult part of this journey is facing the parts of ourselves we've buried or ignored.

For years, I tried to bury specific childhood experiences, convincing myself that some traumas didn't need to be acknowledged, let alone shared. It was easier to believe that if I didn't confront these painful memories, I could move forward untouched. But in disconnecting from my past, I unknowingly disconnected from myself.

The more I tried to silence those wounds, the louder the disconnect became. Looking around, I saw the impact—loved ones drifting away, relationships suffering, and isolation I never intended. I became a stranger to myself, trapped in a cycle of self-denial and unable to build real connections. I held everything in, believing it made me appear strong, yet inside, I felt broken.

The walls I put up to protect myself were the same ones keeping others out.

Genuine connection, however, requires vulnerability—with ourselves and others. Only when I acknowledged my brokenness did I realize the truth: strength doesn't lie in withholding our pain; it lies in confronting it. To build relationships rooted in trust and authenticity, I had to first reconnect with myself, accepting the parts of me I had long avoided.

This journey is more than just self-reflection; it's about embodying the change necessary to foster relationships, about doing the inner work that allows us to be fully present with others. It's a process of learning to let go of fear—the fear of judgment, appearing weak, or being misunderstood—and instead embracing our imperfections with grace.

In doing so, I found my purpose. I realized that my struggles, my journey through vulnerability and reconnection, had given me a unique insight into what it means to truly connect with others. My passion lies in being the bridge—the intervention that helps others truly understand the art of connection.

It's not just about teaching others to open up; it's about showing them that vulnerability is not a weakness but a powerful tool for healing and building deep and meaningful relationships. I want to help people rediscover the truth that connection is the key to everything: love, trust, and growth.

LOST INNOCENCE

My incredible mom was a single parent doing everything she could to make ends meet. At three years old and as an only child, I was surrounded by a loving, extended family. Mom worked full-time and found what seemed to be a safe, reliable babysitter—a woman with children of her own. This arrangement felt like a secure place for my mom to leave her only child.

But it was anything but safe.

While with this woman, I endured things a child should never experience. For privacy, I'll refer to this person as "Jessica." While this part of my story is difficult to share, it's important to understand how those early experiences forever altered the course of my life.

As I write this, I reflect on my eighteen years in law enforcement, a career I dreamed of from a very young age. I always knew I wanted to be a 'cop.' Most people who choose to go into law enforcement will tell you it's something they felt called to do, often from a young age. It's a career that demands bravery, knowing full well the risks involved, including the possibility of injury or even death.

For me, I guess you could say it was a calling, too, but my path was shaped, in part, by Jessica.

For much of my third year of life, Jessica was my babysitter. At that age, our memories are usually fragmented and unclear. But the trauma Jessica inflicted on me remains vivid like it happened yesterday. She liked to do a few things that had lasting effects on me.

Talking about these experiences isn't easy. Through deep therapy and personal reflection, I've learned that to heal, but to do so I must revisit the trauma in my mind. Discussing the painful details of what happened is something none of us want to do. It's easy to convince ourselves that it'll disappear if we bury it deep enough.

I am here as living proof that burying trauma only leads to more pain and that facing it can lead to a life far better than you ever imagined. I'm ready to open up about my earliest traumas with Jessica. I'm ready to show that despite being victimized—and perhaps because of it—you can eventually find gratitude for the journey you're on, even when it's painful.

As a little girl at my babysitter's house, there was a time I had put makeup on a doll and added a little to my face to match—something any young girl might do in the innocence of play. It was a harmless act; a small expression of creativity and fun. But in Jessica's home, this simple act wasn't allowed.

What should have been a moment of joy was instead punished. She dragged me into the bathroom to scrub the makeup off my doll, as if erasing any trace of my innocence. Then she pressed my face into the sink, holding me under the water.

I remember the overwhelming panic of water in my face and the inability to understand why it was happening. The harshness of her actions silenced my cries or any attempt to escape. There was a deep sense of helplessness; a realization that no matter how much I struggled, I was trapped in that moment.

But perhaps what haunts me most isn't just the fear or the pain, but the sound of her laugh—cold and detached, as if she were watching a scene unfold with no empathy or remorse. It was a laugh that didn't reflect joy but a twisted sense of satisfaction as she 'taught me a lesson' I would never forget.

Jessica enjoyed putting a plate in front of me with nothing on it while the other children ate their meals around the table. The plate sat there empty, a silent reminder of how little I mattered.

I felt the hollow feeling of abandonment, being excluded, and being made invisible.

It wasn't as terrifying as the suffocating terror of being held underwater in the bathroom sink, but in its own way, it hurt just as deeply. The isolation I felt during those moments was something worse than hunger; it was the sting of betrayal.

There I was, given nothing, while others were fed and nurtured, as though I didn't deserve the same care or consideration. The emptiness on that plate mirrored the emptiness inside me—the deep, aching wound that Jessica seemed to enjoy reopening time and time again.

One of the most terrifying things Jessica would subject me to was the dreaded closet time-outs. At the back of her house, there was a walk-in closet that quickly became a place of pure dread.

Whenever she decided I had done something wrong, she would

force me inside, making me sit on the cold floor in the middle of the small space while the door slammed shut behind me. The light switch was outside, beyond my reach, leaving me helpless in the dark.

For her amusement, she occasionally flicked the light off and on, adding to the fear, but most of the time, I was left in complete darkness, alone with my racing thoughts.

I gathered the courage to try to open the door just a little, but I quickly discovered it was either locked or barricaded in some way, leaving me completely trapped. No matter how much I struggled, I couldn't escape. I was at the mercy of her decisions, waiting for her to decide when I had "learned my lesson."

In those agonizing moments, I remember thinking that at least I wasn't being held underwater, or at least I wasn't being starved. A three-year-old child can't fully comprehend or process such cruelty, but somehow, I began to measure my suffering, ranking each torment in my mind as though one was less awful than the other.

Looking back, one of the hardest truths to face in my healing journey was realizing that, as a child, the person I feared the most—the one I desperately wanted to escape from—was the very person I had to rely on every day.

She was my babysitter; the adult I was supposed to trust to protect and care for me. Yet, she was the one causing me the most pain and torment. Over time, I unknowingly developed a warped sense of dependency on people or things that, deep down, I knew were unhealthy for me.

Even though I recognized the harm, I couldn't bring myself to break free from them. It's only now, years later, that I can see this pattern and begin the difficult healing process.

HEALING FROM TRAUMA

It wasn't until I was in my twenties that a flood of memories resurfaced—memories of the abuse at Jessica's hands that I had somehow buried deep within me. At the time, I was undergoing hypnosis therapy to address my severe claustrophobia, which had become increasingly debilitating. What I eventually realized was that those 'closet time-outs' were the root cause; a catalyst that planted the seeds of a fear I still struggle with today.

When the memories of the abuse came rushing back, I wasn't ready. In truth, I don't think anyone is ever truly ready to face something like that. Sometimes, I wish those memories had stayed buried—that my mind had kept them locked away forever. Those moments, though long past, left scars that still affect me. A part of me will always wish I had never had to remember, and yet facing it has been a crucial step in my healing journey.

Growing up, I attended the same school as Jessica's children, constantly reminding me of everything I had endured. Children are remarkably resilient, and once I was away from Jessica's influence, I grew up in a healthier, happier environment. Still, seeing her and her kids regularly was never easy.

One day in sixth grade, I walked past Jessica at school. She was with her children, and I seized the moment to confront her. I remember saying something like, "I remember everything you did to me."

The rest of the conversation escaped me, but I felt a surge of pride for having spoken up at all.

That evening, Jessica came to my house to talk to my mom about it. I can still picture her standing in our living room as a flood of painful memories rushed back. My mom had no idea what had happened, so when Jessica made it clear she didn't appreciate my words, my mom decided it was time to have a conversation with me.

Once Jessica left, my mom did what any caring parent would— she sat me down to ask about it. I didn't offer many details, but I made sure to make it clear that Jessica had abused me.

My mom was furious and wanted to take action and confront Jessica herself, but ultimately, she decided that wasn't the best choice.

At that time, I kept most of the details to myself, holding everything in, so my mom never fully understood the depth of what I'd gone through. After that conversation, seeing Jessica or her children became a rare occurrence, and eventually, they faded from my life.

I never spoke of Jessica again or the details of the things she did to me until much later in life. As a child, I was told to keep them secret—and that's exactly what I did. I buried the pain, the fear, and the confusion deep inside, carrying it silently for years.

Putting these experiences into words and allowing them to exist outside of my mind has been both challenging and freeing. I've spoken about it publicly before, but never in writing—never in a way that would memorialize it forever. I share my story now, hoping it reaches others who have walked a similar path. If you've been holding onto something in silence, I want you to know that facing it, as hard as it may be, can set you free. Healing is possible, and you are not alone.

At five years old, I filled out a piece of paper in school—one of those simple worksheets with questions about my favorite color, favorite food, and who my best friend was. And the big one: What do you want to be when you grow up?

My answer? "I want to be a COP."

Looking back now, through the lens of healing, forgiveness, and growth, I've come to see my experiences with Jessica as events that, in some way, happened for a reason. I don't forgive her. She was never held accountable for what she did to me, and even now—thirty-seven years later—I would love nothing more than to see her face justice.

But the reality is, the best thing I can do is reframe my story. I choose to see those painful experiences as the driving force behind a successful career in law enforcement—one that allowed me to protect others and, most importantly, to protect myself from ever being victimized again.

CROSSROADS

In 2020, the divide between law enforcement and our communities was at an all-time high. Situations around the country created a divide that made me feel at home every time I went to work. I had faced many tragedies and challenges, but for the first time, I felt truly discontent with my chosen career path. I was disappointed. I felt as though many people no longer had a sense of safety when we showed up in uniform.

As an empath, I feel things deeply, often to the point of being overwhelmed. Over time, I've learned to manage those emotions, even controlling the flow of tears that used to come so easily. But the tenderhearted person within me hasn't disappeared. That part of me is still there, requiring effort—not just from me, but from those who share my daily life. I imagine it can be taxing sometimes to be around someone who feels everything so intensely.

Being an empath is a gift. It's a beautiful quality that connects us to the world and others in meaningful ways. It may take work, but it's a strength worth embracing.

During the summer of 2020, I realized I was becoming someone no one wanted to be around—someone I didn't even recognize. It was as if I had reached the edge of a cliff, and one more step in the wrong direction would take me somewhere from which I couldn't return. One day of emotional and mental negativity led to the next. I couldn't see my way out of this cycle, but that empath inside me knew I had to find a way. I woke up one day and decided enough was enough.

I must give credit where it's due—God would not let me continue down this path. Speaking with mentors over the years, I've come to call my awakening a download from God. I wanted to find a way to bring people back together. I had grandiose ideas of changing the world, but it started small. I kept brainstorming what the world needed. How would I be the light in this dark cycle we were all experiencing? How could I bring people back together? I had to CONNECT them. My download was just beginning. Connection was required, and I intended to be the vessel to express the message God was giving me.

CONNECT was born—not as a tool for me, but to teach others. Little did I realize it would later become a lifeline for myself. CONNECT has now become more than a simple concept; it's a testament to the power of rebuilding, finding strength in vulnerability, and trusting that our darkest moments can lead us to our greatest purpose.

How often in our lives do we feel like everything is going wrong? When this happens, we can find ourselves overwhelmed with anger, bitterness, and sadness. At this crossroads, we have choices. We can either choose to remain in this discontent, fully aware that nothing positive can arise from it, or we can acknowledge that the power to change lies within us. While this realization may seem straightforward when condensed into a single paragraph, the reality is far more complex. Choosing to change also involves embracing a deep sense of self-awareness.

Coming to terms with the fact that, in most cases, we are the biggest obstacle in our way can be a harsh realization. While there are times when we are actual victims, we still have control over one crucial aspect: our thoughts. Life happens. Circumstances beyond our control create unavoidable realities. What we do control is how we respond. When we accept that most of life is shaped by our reactions to events rather than the events themselves, we begin to reclaim our power. Once you fully embrace this perspective, it can be transformative.

Without my experiences, I may never have received the incredible blessing from God to bring my model, CONNECT, into the world—a mission that now helps others find healing, purpose, and strength in their own lives.

How can you apply CONNECT to your own life?

CONNECT is more than just a concept—it's a framework, a mindset, and a powerful tool designed to help you bridge the gap between where you are and where you want to be. It's about fostering genuine relationships, embracing vulnerability, and taking intentional steps toward growth and healing.

Through CONNECT, I've learned how to transform setbacks into stepping-stones and to build a life rooted in resilience and authenticity.

Whether you're looking to strengthen personal relationships, overcome past challenges, or simply find clarity in your purpose, CONNECT provides practical strategies to guide you forward.

CONNECT is the model for the seven pillars required for successful human relationships:

- Communication
- Openness
- Neutrality
- Nurturing
- Education
- Courage
- Transparency

When we take the time to truly understand and connect with ourselves, we create a solid foundation for personal growth and emotional well-being. This self-awareness allows us to recognize our own needs, values, and boundaries, which in turn helps us navigate our interactions with others more thoughtfully and empathetically. By cultivating a deeper connection with ourselves, we are better equipped to show up as our authentic selves in relationships, fostering trust, understanding, and meaningful connections. We'll never reach a final destination where we can just check it off and move on. This way of living requires daily dedication for as long as we walk this Earth.

Finding myself has been a journey I didn't expect to take. My life has shifted in ways I never anticipated, mainly because of my own mistakes—mistakes I wish I could undo. I've had to face the consequences of those mistakes head-on. Failed relationships, broken trust, and wounded hearts brought me to a place where change became inevitable. I realized I was on a path that had no return if I didn't make a shift. Today, I stand as the most potent version of myself I've ever been. I've reconnected with who I truly am, and through that, I can connect with the right people and the right path for the rest of my life.

Genuine connection is not only possible, but it's something that can be cultivated with intention. In my journey toward healing, I have discovered a profound sense of purpose that didn't exist before. The painful memories of my early childhood are slowly becoming just that—memories rather than defining aspects of who I am. But I've realized that the healing journey is ongoing; it's never really 'complete.' The scars remain, and they always will, but they no longer control me.

I don't believe these experiences are things we can—or should—forget. I'm not asking you to forget your painful moments, either.

It's not about erasing them from our lives. Instead, we focus on healing in a way that allows us to be at peace with those memories. The goal is to stop being paralyzed by them. We can acknowledge them without letting them define our present when they resurface.

The actual work begins within, through honest communication with ourselves. When we connect with ourselves compassionately and truthfully, we begin to build the foundation for deeper, more meaningful connections with others. Through this inner work, we can embrace vulnerability, trust, and authenticity in our relationships. The path to connection isn't about perfection; it's about learning to be present, even when the past makes an appearance.

Ultimately, healing is not a linear process, nor is it one-size-fits-all. It's messy, it's uncomfortable, and it's often filled with setbacks. But the beauty lies in our capacity to grow and reconnect with ourselves and others in new, more honest ways. True healing is not about erasing the past—it's about learning to live with it, accept it, and use it as a stepping-stone to becoming the person we are meant to be. And in doing so, we open ourselves up to the possibility of profound connection, both with ourselves and those around us.

The path to connection isn't about perfection; it's about learning to be present, even when the past makes an appearance.

"I AM LOVED."
By Lacey Nelson

LACEY NELSON BIOGRAPHY

Lacey Nelson, a Sacramento native, earned her bachelor's degree in criminal justice from California State University, Sacramento in 2009. While working for the Sacramento County Probation Department, Lacey pursued her dream of becoming a law enforcement officer.

In 2012, she was hired by a Northern California Sheriff's Office, where she has since served in various roles, including in correctional facilities, the Media and Community Relations Division, and patrol. Lacey now holds the rank of sergeant.

Lacey continued her education by earning a master's degree from Pennsylvania State University in 2022. Her passion for community involvement led her to run for a seat on her local water district, where she has served as a director since November 2020 and was re-elected in 2024.

In addition to her law enforcement career, Lacey is a public speaker and the founder of CONNECT, a business dedicated to helping people build deeper, more meaningful relationships. She has appeared on television and radio to promote her work and currently hosts the CONNECT podcast, which is available on her social media channels. Lacey also volunteers with 93Q Radio.

Lacey is driven by a commitment to make a positive, lasting impact.

CONNECT WITH LACEY.

Website: www.laceynelson.com
Email: Lacey@Laceynelson.com
Follow on Socials: IG @lacey__nelson, FB @laceylace0722, TT @the_lacey_nelson

CHAPTER 6

THROUGH THE SHADOWS
BACK TO THE LIGHT

**"When you master your relationship with Self, you
master your relationship with others."**

By Judy M. Graybill

*"Through the Shadows Back to the Light" by Judy Graybill is a journey
of resilience, heart healing, and transformation. A quest to be happy
and a profound dream catalyzes her Healing Journey and Spiritual
Awakening, creating a strong foundation to overcome many hurdles:
financial hardship, mental health struggles, family conflict, profound
grief, and the weight of responsibility.*

*When all outcomes seemed undesirable, she made tough choices with
unwavering personal integrity. Fueled by a commitment to rebuild
broken familial connections amidst the heartbreaking reality of caring
for a mother with Alzheimer's, she weaved into being a stronger support system and renewed sense of self. This chapter is a testament to the
power of being intentional in word and deed while being true to yourself.*

THROUGH THE SHADOWS
BACK TO THE LIGHT

I woke up in a sweat, my heart palpitating feverishly, raw jealousy and anger pulsing through me. Just a dream, thank goodness. But it felt so real! My ex was there, along with his toxic ex. Obviously, it's related to the biggest heartbreak of my life—my dysfunctional stepfamily experience. The heaviness of it loomed over me like a storm cloud that could burst open any minute with torrential rainfall. What did it mean?

Could this be an answer to my quest? Just the night before, I prayed to the ethers for help. *Prayed? Well, more like soulful pleading.* Tired of the constant pain, I longed for inner peace. From the depths of my being, I made an energetic decision that I would be happy again, although I had no clue how. Not having any faith in God at the time, I didn't have any expectations. Mere hours later, this dream happened. I felt like it contained the essence of a profound message, and I set out to decode it.

RE-SHAPING MY REFLECTION

For the next several years, I spent most of my spare time reading, profoundly expanding my point of view—philosophically, mentally, emotionally, and spiritually—pushing myself to dig deeper into understanding myself better. "Know thyself, and thou shalt know the universe," a Greek philosophical maxim, became a personal motif.

I started journaling as a form of meditation. That helped me to recognize unhealthy thought patterns so I could reprogram them. I realized that everything I experienced was an opportunity to understand myself more intricately. I made sense of the underlying reasons for my choices, thus shifting my ability to choose more conscientiously. I learned how to weed out toxic people and steer away from dysfunctional situations. Gradually, my outlook brightened. Once again, I felt empowered and capable of creating a happy life. As an unexpected side effect, it awakened an appreciation for spiritual living. To wit, I had a Spiritual Awakening.

My heart expanded in ways I had never experienced before. I felt propelled by a desire to help step-couples stay together instead of separating out of hopelessness as I had done. I became a certified stepfamily coach and started my company, Sensible Steps. Surprisingly, I got clients who experienced worse conflict than me. As challenging as that was, my past experience transformed into a silver lining. It gave me the insight I needed to adequately assess my clients' problems, teach new tools for effective communication, and share a healthy model of stepfamily life. I still remember my first clients telling me that I gave them peace of mind because they no longer argued after a long day of work. It's such an exquisitely fulfilling feeling to be able to help others. This gratitude uplifted me from many low points as I struggled to build my business into a profitable career as a single woman.

WHEN SHADOWS COME TO LIGHT

I wish I could say that my newfound spirituality was enough to create a life that was smooth sailing. However, that was not the case. Four years after separating from my ex, I was still trying to recover my financial losses and heal from the acute dysfunction. With no money in the bank and my credit in ruins, all my money went toward essentials like rent and food. So, I moved back to Phoenix, Arizona, to be near family and a stronger support system. An ex-boyfriend with whom I maintained a close friendship had extra space in his home and offered it to me rent-free until I got back on my feet. That provided me with the stability I needed to focus my full attention on growing my coaching business through my ongoing healing journey.

Any goal worth achieving will push you out of your comfort zone. Inherent in the journey are trials that expose your vulnerabilities, even if only to yourself. Queue the next predicament. Severe panic attacks came out of nowhere, so debilitating that it took all my energy just to make one phone call or write an email. They were residual effects of complex trauma caused by past toxic situations. Healing it required a deeper level of self-discovery. It also required time, patience, and grit. That translated to minimal work production, gradually increasing to a full workload over a two-year period.

After regaining my confidence, I made the bold decision to host a telesummit for stepfamilies. It was going to be my big comeback! I spent innumerable hours on the project: I formed a small mastermind to brainstorm ideas, lined up sixteen speakers, bought a domain name, wrote website copy, gathered giveaways, and looked for sponsors. Once again, I was excited about life!

It all came to a crashing halt on Friday, October 25, 2013. A friend was coming over to record me doing an intro video for the registration page. I had stayed up to the wee hours of the morning memorizing the script. I felt ready and awaited for his arrival with nervous anticipation. I took a quick Facebook break. That's when

I saw the horrifying "In memory of . . ." photo post of my niece. *What the . . . ?! This must be a mistake (a scam maybe)?* Shocked and confused, I immediately called my sister, Jan. Her significant other answered, apparently fielding a flood of calls. It was true! Early that morning, my niece's ex had broken into her house and shot her. She died a couple of hours later at the hospital.

That fateful day changed the course of the next six years. Not just for Jan, but for Mom, who had been living with Jan after her recent diagnosis of Alzheimer's, and for me, who would become Mom's power of attorney (POA).

CHOOSING MY LIGHT WITHIN

I was the one who first posited the idea of establishing a POA. It was the strong advice I got through my self-education process of learning to care for an Alzheimer's patient. It was one of many things that needed to be discussed and decided upon related to Mom, and that called for a family meeting. My sisters and I started meeting weekly via my telephone conference line. Brenda and Sandra, my two eldest sisters, opted out for personal reasons. That left Jan, Tess, Mallory, and me. When the subject of establishing a POA came up, I was taken aback when both Mallory and Jan wanted to do it, just as I did. Their desire to help and be included, I understood. What surprised and confused me, though, was the ferocity with which Mallory expressed the desire for it to be her. More to the point, for it to not be me. She didn't have a problem with Jan being POA—only me, although she preferred herself over Jan. We found ourselves in a tenuous impasse, week after week, for almost four months.

How did it come to this? So clearly I remembered the days of having fun together. Sure, we fought like all siblings did, but most were menial squabbles. The good times, on the other hand, bonded us together. Like when we formed the Secret Trio Club (STC) as young kids. We wrote full skits and singing acts, including costumes, to perform for Mom and Dad. After Mom and Dad split, we pulled our money together to buy Christmas gifts for Mom and Grandma. Oh the look of surprise when we revealed a few unknown presents from "Santa!" Long gone were those days. What happened to the essence of the STC?

I kinda understood Jan, Sandra, and Brenda not feeling close to Tess, Mallory, and me, because we didn't grow up together. As older half-siblings, they were already out of the house when I was born. Yet, I couldn't seem to shake not getting any notice about my niece. The words of Jan's significant other lingered in my mind. When I asked if he wanted help calling the family, he said, "All the family's been called."

What? What do you mean? I thought. *I'm family. I wasn't called. Tess and Mallory weren't called.*

How did our relationship turn into a non-relationship? When did we stop trusting each other? Instead of collaborating on potential solutions, we're having a power struggle over who Mom's POA should be.

The irony was that I didn't really want the responsibility. I was barely getting back on my feet and needed to nurture my business for it to proliferate. Plus, I still had hopes of resuming my telesummit for stepfamilies. My choice to volunteer as POA was neither rash nor from a wounded ego. Quite the contrary. I thought long and hard and re-evaluated many times. I kept coming back to the conclusion that it made the most sense for it to be me. Jan was too mired in her grief. Mallory lived out-of-state, which precluded her ability to be effective. Plus, she worked a demanding schedule at the hospital. If she were local, it'd be a no-brainer, especially since she vehemently wanted to do it. However, in the current circumstances, it was moot. I was the only one who was not only local but also had the flexibility of forming my own hours. Little did I know that the flexibility required would push me to my near-breaking point.

Here we were, queens of our own castles and primary decision-makers, without a clue how to work together as a team. Quitting was not an option. Not for me, and obviously not for my sisters. What to do? The only thing I could do was leave it in God's hands. After years of spiritual development, I had complete trust that God would right this ship for Mom's highest interest, as long as we allowed Him to. I knew in my heart that the only thing I needed to do was assert what I wanted and let God do the rest. That's the day I made two decisions:

1. I wasn't going to push, force, or fight. I'd be true to my own opinions of what I thought was best and clearly state it aloud. Then, I'd step back and allow the chips to fall where they may. In other words, I let go and let God.

2. I wanted a good relationship with my sisters, and decided I would do everything I could to cultivate a team environment.

Those two decisions colored every subsequent decision for the next five years, altering the trajectory of the journey we'd walk together as sisters as we simultaneously grieved the loss of our Mom, each in our own way. Shortly thereafter, Jan made the profound choice to withdraw her request. After much soul-searching, praying, and the help of her support system, she finally realized the importance of focusing on her grieving—that it's not only okay to put herself first, but that she wouldn't be letting Mom down in the process. Next, both Jan and Tess opined to Mallory that the role of POA couldn't be as effective out-of-state. To assure Mallory that I wouldn't go rogue as a controlling b****, I instituted the majority vote rule and gave my word that I'd implement whatever we collectively decided regardless of my personal views. It felt right to do it that way, and I figured it was the only way to alleviate her concerns. Although it took a couple more weeks, Mallory hesitantly conceded. Thus, I became Mom's POA.

The first three years were fairly easy because I knew Mom was happy. That's when she impetuously repeated the same few sentiments like a broken record: how blessed she was to have such wonderful kids, how God had been good to her, and how everybody is so nice. Once, when we were driving to an appointment, a wave of aggravation hit me as I longed to have a real conversation. I heartily missed my mom. Suddenly, I had an epiphany, like a message from Spirit. Her 'broken record' was a tone of gratitude—not anger, paranoia, nor any sort of mean outbursts that most family members in my shoes dealt with. Immediately, my irritation turned into sunshine. It never bothered me again.

RESPECTING THE SHADOWS TO HONOR THE REFLECTION

Eventually, the day came when she wasn't happy—the day she could no longer walk on her own. At that time, her sadness was in brief moments here or there. However, I could see that Mom had to work at being positive. Her boyfriend was a daily mood brightener. He was always around because he was another resident. That gave me some comfort. At the same time, it took increasingly more effort to get Mom to smile for the camera—a stark difference to the ham she used to be. This, unfortunately, marked her steep decline.

This is when the real work began; when the challenges multiplied quickly without resolution. If I alone was the decision-maker, it would have been easier. But nope, I was constantly battling the administrators and care-givers at the home to do what they said they would do. On top of that, whenever my sisters outvoted me on a decision, I felt like I had to choose between my relationship with them and my Mom's health. I stuck with my commitment to them, but it haunted me. I wondered if my decisions were pushing Mom closer to the grave.

A couple of friends told me they would override their siblings' votes if it was best for their parent, as part of their 'duty' as POA. *But that means going back on my word! I came a long way in rebuilding their trust in me. I can't bring myself to go backward,* I thought. My conscience battled internally. Knowing (and doing) what you have to do is one thing. Facing the reality of that action is quite another. It was a lose-lose situation.

It was more than an agreement to my sisters; It was a commitment to myself as well. It was important to me to once again have a strong sisterly relationship. I had to look myself in the mirror every night. If I didn't have my integrity, who was I? Could I live with the ramifications of my decisions? How could I make peace with my Soul?

The worst of it? Watching a person you love dwindle into nothing. It's bad enough to lose Mom as I once knew her, but I had to watch my once vibrant, strong, independent mother digress into a frail helpless woman who couldn't walk, didn't talk, and became bedridden. At each stage, I mourned the loss of my Mom, over and over again.

I lamented the role of POA and all it entailed. My grieving process was made worse by this burdensome responsibility. To think how naive I was in the beginning when I thought I'd only be writing checks and talking to a few medical professionals. There was so much to do that I could hardly keep up. Actually, I didn't. I once balled my eyes out to Tess after she had casually alerted me to Mom's ingrown toenails, totally unaware of my failed attempts to get her a podiatrist. I felt like a complete failure—to my mom, my sisters, and to myself. My tears weren't about the podiatrist, though. It was the heavy weight of everything that I couldn't protect Mom from. Through my tears, I tried to explain all the things going wrong: nine months of fighting the insurance company to approve Mom's replacement dentures, nine months of trying to get the care home to soften Mom's food so she could still chew it, nine months of her losing weight because she wasn't eating enough, and over three years of the care home administrators saying they would do things that never got done. Add to that all the doctor appointments that they neglected to tell me about or would allow to happen in my absence when the time changed, and then making decisions on my/Mom's behalf without my consent, constantly losing Mom's clothes, not notifying me when she needed more shampoo or other essentials, and the list went on. More was being thrown at me with each passing month.

Nobody else could possibly grasp the intricacies of this responsibility. The toll it puts on the mind, heart, and body is a uniquely heart-wrenching experience that only caregivers and POAs can truly understand. Plus, finding time to work on my coaching business became increasingly problematic. Even when I had time, my heart wasn't in it. I didn't have the mental capacity to concentrate. Physical energy? Forget it! All I wanted to do was take a nap.

RE-IGNITING MY SPARK

As Mom's Alzheimer's progressed to the final stages, her needs increased significantly. I did what I had to do despite the pain in my heart. My energy depleted and creative spark too dim to work, I faced a quandary of how to be productive. After some contemplation, it occurred to me that preparing for the inevitable could be healthy productivity. I grimaced at the thought of doing it alone. So I asked Tess to help me pre-plan Mom's funeral. She quickly and graciously agreed, and then we checked in with Jan and Mallory. No objections.

During the six years on this journey together—through all the discussions/disagreements, Mom's hospital visits, and reaching across the divide—we found the pieces that connected us. It was our love for Mom and the pain of losing her. We started recognizing and honoring each other's individual relationship with her, which showed up as acute sensitivity to specific topics. Instead of pushing harder, we saw beneath the pain. After my breakdown, Tess gave me a bouquet of flowers as an expression of gratitude for all I was doing for Mom. In conversations with Jan, I felt understood and validated. When Mallory got out-voted, her emotional struggle paralleled mine. When I wasn't able to console her, Jan filled the gap. Alas, Mallory defended me to the funeral director after miscommunications and confusion regarding Mom's commemoration book. We were finally communicating like sisters. I know the reason is because I set that precedent through my intentional decisions, and then allowing God's light to do the rest. I kept my word in all I did. I had slip-ups, of course, due to the overwhelm, but I owned up to them sincerely while putting my best foot forward.

Gratitude filled my heart for not having to do the rest alone. The bonus was the bonding experience with Tess when we created a commemorative bookmark to give away at Mom's funeral. Because she was an avid reader, this made the perfect memento to celebrate her life. We made it out of a hug coupon that Mom sent out in every birthday card. Each bookmark was laminated with a hand-written "In memory of . . ." note on the back.

When Mom passed, all six of us daughters came together to make Mom's final celebration of life an enjoyable family experience. My only wish is that it would've lasted longer. There was only one detail left to work out: Mom's expensive hand-carved ivory rosary. She wanted it buried with her, but it was too big to fit in the urn or niche. After a bit of deliberation, we unanimously decided to send it to Mallory, who ardently expressed a desire for it. Her feeling of loss was intensified due to the 2,000-mile distance. Although the rosary couldn't make up for that, we hoped that it could at least bring her comfort and help her feel closer to Mom.

Once the weight of responsibility for Mom's life was lifted, my true healing began. Knowing that Mom was finally in a state of true peace was the first stepping-stone. The second was my sisterly relationship. There's a comfort among us that didn't exist in the beginning, and I think Mom would be proud of us for how we rose to support each other. After all, we are seeded from her, the best role model.

I'm no stranger to the Healing Journey. Starting with my decision to be happy after the fateful enigmatic dream, this leg of it extended a lesson beyond mental understanding. There's always unanswered questions, such as why unfortunate events happen or some people don't act cooperatively (such as the administrators and caregivers). Every single one of us gets to choose our own path. While I can't speak to others' choices, especially when they seem discordant with the collective good, I am proud to say that I've made peace with mine. I know it's not the outcome that matters most, but rather how we travel our path. Staying in integrity with my values enriched my life. When I look in the mirror, I smile at my reflection. I see the growth. I like who I am, and who I am becoming. My journey of the soul continues.

At the end of the day, you have to look at yourself in the mirror. What do you want your reflection to illuminate? You get to decide.

"I AM A SPARK OF THE DIVINE ON A JOURNEY OF SELF-DISCOVERY."
By Judy M Graybill

JUDY M GRAYBILL BIOGRAPHY

Judy M. Graybill is a seasoned transformational relationship healer and certified stepfamily coach dedicated to helping couples and individuals transform unhealthy relationship patterns into loving connections. With twenty years of experience in high-conflict situations, remarriages, and relationships affected by complex trauma, Judy helps clients identify and address the root causes of conflict, empowering them with tools to rebuild trust and strengthen partnerships. Her trauma-informed approach, founded in practical spirituality and soul-centered healing, guides clients through a four-step transformational journey of self-discovery and heart-healing into becoming happier, more confident, and naturally open to fulfilling experiences.

Judy's formal degrees in sociology and psychology, and multiple certifications, are complemented by her personal healing journey. A child of divorce, she has firsthand knowledge of dysfunctional family patterns. They followed her into adulthood and four failed relationships, culminating in a painful but amicable ending to her high-conflict stepfamily experience. Feeling heartbroken, confused, and resentful, Judy set out to be happy and whole again. Through a personal and spiritual journey, she healed her complex trauma without traditional therapy, igniting her passion to help others through similar experiences.

In addition to coaching, she speaks, writes, and facilitates in-person workshops.

CONNECT WITH JUDY:
Email: hello@judygraybill.com
Website: www.judygraybill.com
Follow on Socials: IG @judy.m.graybil, FB @judygraybill, LI @judygraybill
#transformationalrelationshiphealer #JudyMGraybill #traumainformed

CHAPTER 7

BREAKING FREE:
LIVING LIMITLESSLY BEYOND THE BOX

**"At some point in our lives, we must pick up
our torch and light our own way."**

By Havilah Malone

Havilah Malone's journey is one of resilience, transformation, and liberation from imposed expectations. In "Breaking Free: Living Limitlessly Beyond the Box," she shares her powerful story—growing up within the strict confines of a highly structured religious environment, enduring childhood trauma, seeking validation through achievements, and navigating the pain of suppressing her inner voice to fit in.

Refusing to live a fragmented life or be defined by her challenges, she embraced a path of deep healing and self-discovery. A life-changing experience—walking on fire at a Tony Robbins retreat—ignited a new sense of courage to live authentically beyond any box, leading her to

* Disclaimers 1, 3, and 4.

travel the world and learn from him and an elite group of enlightened entrepreneurs. Through it all, she discovered the true power of personal transformation, allowing her to shine even brighter. Her message is both inspiring and profound: "We must pick up our torch and light our own way, giving ourselves the things we need to thrive."

BREAKING FREE:
LIVING LIMITLESSLY BEYOND THE BOX

I walked on FIRE! An event that changed the trajectory of my life. It was 2012 in Orlando, Florida. I sat wide-eyed in anticipation as a 6-foot-6 man spoke with such fervor and passion about the power we possess within and how we could unleash it. With every word that left his lips and landed at the base of my hearing, I knew he was right.

I was destined to be in that room, receiving every message Tony Robbins delivered. But there was one big problem. Simply being there was breaking every rule I had ever known, and I was probably going to catch hell for it.

There is no greater act of self-love than to follow your own internal guidance and carve out a path that is uniquely yours.

Over 5,000 attendees filed out of the massive auditorium ready to put Tony's captivating teachings to the test. As I watched the smoke rise and listened to the crackling of fiery coals, I took a deep breath. Looking straight ahead, I began chanting a mantra as onlookers cheered me on. With each barefoot step, swift and precise, I walked across burning embers—unscathed. Not one scratch. Not one bruise. Not one burn. Pretty miraculous, right?

How did I get to this place? How did I unlock this ability? And why would I even experiment with such a dangerous act?

MY PERFECTLY POLISHED BOX

Growing up in Southern Louisiana, I was surrounded by my parents' love. My mom's job as an international flight attendant allowed our family to travel the world, experiencing different cultures and perspectives. But there's always a box waiting for us—one we can contort ourselves into to fit the mold. The box of religion. The family box. The school box. The societal expectation box.

Mine was a neat, perfectly polished box—one that provided safety, community, and a deep sense of shared purpose and belonging. As a Jehovah's Witness, theocratic activities filled our lives five days a week. Tuesday nights were dedicated to theocratic ministry school and service meetings. Thursday nights, we gathered for Bible study. Saturday mornings we knocked on doors in field service, and Sundays were spent at morning meetings, followed by more field service.

Even our 'free' days weren't truly free. Mondays and Wednesdays were set aside for at-home study, preparing for all the meetings we were expected to attend. It was a well-oiled machine—one that provided stability and plenty to keep our minds and time occupied as we waited for God to bring an end to this world's corrupt system of things.

We didn't celebrate holidays like Christmas or birthdays. I remember a Valentine's Day event in elementary school when my mom checked me and my older brother out early. I felt a little sad, thinking I'd miss out on the tasty heart-shaped treats. But as we got into Mom's van, I saw it was filled with bags of candy—just for us. She was always so thoughtful, making sure we never felt left out.

Our family believed that through obedience to our religious beliefs and unwavering faith in God's word, we would be saved from destruction and granted the opportunity to live forever in a Paradise on Earth.

Whose dream was this?

Deep down, I had no desire to live forever. I had a feeling I'd done this many times before.

As a little girl, I desired self-expression. I loved to twirl around the living room, singing and dancing. I'd use my hairbrush and pretend to interview imaginary people while delivering the news on TV. There was something so liberating about this act that allowed all my gifts to shine brightly, but whenever someone walked into the room, I stopped. I didn't want to be seen.

I loved my family deeply, and I knew they loved me. But nothing on this Earth truly felt like home. I'd go outside and lay on the warm, paved concrete of our driveway. Staring into the vast, beautiful blue sky with a longing gaze, tears streamed down my face. Desperately, I tried to peer beyond the clouds, searching for meaning. Wondering where I truly came from. Where did I belong?

I believed that if I asked God, He would reveal my true identity—that maybe I had been dropped off here on Earth or had accidentally fallen out of the sky, and He was coming back to get me, to bring me to my real home.

Why couldn't I just fit in and think like everyone else? Why did I have to be such a weirdo?

Did I choose this, or was it chosen for me?

THE PROGRAMMING

We were taught that our religious teachings were the truth. But isn't the truth supposed to set you free? Whose truth? Why did I feel so boxed in?

I always admired elderly people—they could say or do whatever they wanted without a care in the world. I loved their ability to just be themselves, regardless of what anyone thought. Living beyond any box takes courage and trust in oneself. The embodiment of those qualities leads to an audacious authenticity and inner power that no one can take from you.

I muffled my inner voice to mirror the voice of the congregation. It was a beautiful voice, but not a reflection of the totality of who I was. I lived in pieces—some parts of me shined, while others stayed hidden deep within, deemed unworthy of seeing the light. There was no one I could talk to about the things I truly wanted to explore.

In middle school, I began writing poetry—just thoughts, ideas, and streams of consciousness that I couldn't express out loud. I wrote them down in my notebook; my safe place of exploration. I didn't consider myself a writer, nor did I think of my writing as poetry. It was simply a way to express myself that no one else would ever see.

At some point in our lives, we must pick up our torch and light our own way. Giving ourselves the things we need to thrive, taking with us the jewels that serve us, and leaving behind the elements that don't.

I had been given a blueprint for my life, so I knew what was important and what I had to do to follow society's rules. But I always looked for a faster, more direct path. If I was going to do something, I wanted to do it my way. I felt like my real life was waiting on the other side of these obligations, and at the moment, the obligation was called school.

I was ahead of my time in many ways—graduating from high school at sixteen and then finishing college by nineteen with two degrees: one in dramatic arts and communication, the other in psychology. I then joined the newsroom at Fox 8 in New Orleans immediately after graduating. By the age of twenty-one, I had entered upper-level management at a Fortune 500 company.

During college, there were two people in my congregation I felt like I could really talk to; we'll just call them Sister V, and Brother H. Everyone in the congregation is referred to as Brother or Sister, as it fosters a sense of familial connection to one another. I always felt drawn to people much older than me. Sister V, my friend's mom, felt like a kindred spirit. Whenever I was at their house, I spent more time talking with her than my friend. She saw and understood me in a way few did, offering wisdom on navigating conflicts with my mom or the emotional disappearing acts of my dad. She listened, made me laugh, and always shared practical advice.

After Bible study, Brother H and I would dive into "what if" conversations—exploring science, history, and Biblical prophecy. What if dinosaurs never went extinct? What if we made it to paradise but sinned again? Our discussions were fascinating and deeply thought-provoking, but the reply to many of my questions was, "We'll know in God's appointed time. Just keep walking in faith."

For my endlessly curious mind, it was an unsatisfying answer. We were only allowed to study materials provided by our religious organization—exploring other religious texts was considered interfaith and, therefore, a sin. The box I lived in was sealed tight, but my soul longed to breathe.

For years, I silenced that voice, pushing it deeper and deeper inside, because who was I to question the authority of this long-standing religious powerhouse and the men ordained to lead it? All men, by the way.

In Matthew 7:7, we're urged, "Keep on asking, and it will be given you; keep on seeking, and you will find; keep on knocking, and it shall be opened to you."

It was time for me to knock a little harder! But if I kicked up too much dust, it may call attention to my big dirty secret.

MY BIG DIRTY SECRET

It was 2006, a year after Hurricane Katrina devastated Louisiana and parts of the southern coastal region. I'd evacuated to Dallas, Texas, and joined a local congregation where I met and began dating a brother who was seventeen years older than me and had spent nearly two decades previously incarcerated. He'd turned his life around and became a Jehovah's Witness. We were introduced by his mother, my masseuse, who'd whisper in my ear during our sessions about her son and how great he was. In this state of relaxation, her constant whispers became more intriguing.

Dating was very serious, only undertaken as a step towards marriage. We were only allowed to date others who shared the same faith, as to remain like-minded and uphold our religious beliefs. One rule of dating was never to be alone with the opposite sex; a shield from temptation and committing immoral acts. Therefore, you were always chaperoned until marriage.

On one occasion, my boyfriend stopped by my apartment to drop something off. During this visit, we were alone. As he was leaving, we embraced in a goodbye kiss, which passionately escalated as his hand slowly slid down my yoga pants and touched my privates. I didn't resist it. I enjoyed it. We both knew it was wrong. We stopped, and he left.

After a few weeks, his conscience began weighing heavily on him. He informed me he was going to confess his sins to the congregation's Elders, a body of men appointed as leaders with oversight roles in the congregation. I was struck with fear. What would the Elders do? What strict judgment would they pass down on us for breaking the rules? Over the following days, I was under a tremendous amount of stress, imagining what my punishment would be for this heinous act of passion.

During this time, I took a trip back home to Louisiana for business and to visit my family. While sitting alone at my mom's house, I kept asking myself and contemplating why I allowed this to happen. *Why, why, why?* And like a flood, this tidal wave of memories all came back. This was not the first time I'd engaged in a sexual act or allowed myself to be violated. This was one of many over the years, originating back to childhood and the very first violation by my brother when I was ten.

He used coercion, manipulation, and threats that made me believe that I would get in trouble if I told anyone. For years, I suppressed those memories, burying them deep in my subconscious mind. I believed there was no place in my perfectly polished box for them to fit or find release. I couldn't talk about it, so I chose not to remember it for most of my life.

These memories came crashing down on me like a ton of bricks; some details blurred, some as clear as day. There were some encounters where I didn't even remember the guys' names. It was so overwhelming and devastating that I wept; a deep soul cry as my body heaved and tears flowed from my eyes until they were swollen and burning. The shame, the guilt, and the disgust were so horrific that I knew the only answer at that moment was to end it all. Then, the pain would stop and the memories would cease to exist.

I went into the bathroom, one of the very same places where my brother had molested me. I began writing a letter to my parents at 12:16 p.m. on October 2, 2006. I thanked them for all their love and support and asked them not to blame themselves for the choice I was about to make. I left behind all my account passwords and instructions on where to find everything they would need after I was gone.

I pulled out a knife I had taken from the kitchen and slid it from the top of my wrist down my vein. But as fate would have it, it wasn't my time to die. The blade was too blunt to pierce the skin. I tried again, applying more force, and it barely scratched the surface. I sobbed even harder as I felt this sense of being held by a divine force in that moment.

After a few hours, I gathered myself and put the letter away. My parents were none the wiser, not finding out about the day they almost lost their daughter and why this tragedy even occurred until nearly eight years later.

After my trip to New Orleans, I returned to Texas to meet with the Elders and confess my sins. During the meeting, I sat at a table surrounded by three brothers from my congregation. They questioned me and asked for a detailed account of what happened between my boyfriend and me. They counseled me, referred to scriptures highlighting the wrongdoing of my actions, and emphasized the need for repentance from this immortality to regain God's favor. I told them everything!

It was humiliating. A violation of my privacy. A recutting of a wound that had not yet healed. But at that moment, I believed that this was a part of God's loving arrangement to protect his people; that this was what must be done.

For my punishment, I was put on public reproof, meaning they read my name from the stage in front of the congregation, alerting them that I'd sinned and had received disciplinary action. Talk about adding trauma to trauma.

After that meeting, many of the Brothers and Sisters in the congregation came up to me and shared that they had been publicly or privately reproved at some point and that everything would be okay. It was like I'd joined this Secret Society of the Scarlet Letter Gang.

As much as everything seemed picture-perfect on the outside, there was so much going on behind the scenes that no one talked about. There was an outpouring of empathy and compassion from many, while others looked at me with disdain. This was the world I lived in. Judge and jury, friends and foes, life and death, all in the power of the Word.

But whose word was it? Is this what God wanted, or was this just man's interpretation of what God wanted? I truly went through the fire, and this wasn't even half of it.

By age twenty-eight, I'd already been married and divorced to a brother in a congregation after moving back to Louisiana. By the time I took the rose-colored glasses off and realized that my betrothed was exceptionally good at living a double life, the lies, deceit, cheating, and fraud were more than I could bear, and I jumped ship. That story is a whole Lifetime movie in itself, so I'll spare you the details!

My faith was waning, my personal life was falling apart, and I still hadn't fully healed from all that had happened. From the outside looking in, you'd never know. I still managed to smile through the pain because this perfectly polished box I lived in required it.

I actively attended congregation meetings, although I was less engaged. I continued to participate in the door-to-door ministry, preaching about God's Kingdom and the destruction of this old system of things. But now, looking back, what I was really preaching about was the destruction of my own internal system of programming.

My beliefs were coming to a breaking point. Not only had I jumped ship from a sham of a marriage, but little did I know I was going to dismantle every limitation that was ever placed on my life and go in search of the real me.

BREAKING OUT OF THE BOX

Career-wise I was thriving. Academic and secular achievements were areas of my life in which I had always thrived. My accomplishments were the shield I wore to protect myself and hide my flaws. In corporate America I was managing a $160 million technology business for one of the largest computer manufacturers in the world, Hewlett-Packard. I'd also become a major public figure on television, selling their products on QVC, HSN, and Shop@HomeTV. During this time, I had the opportunity to star in a reality show and even launched my acting career.

Overachieving was an understatement, but that was a part of my mask. Behind all of these achievements was an immense amount of pain and fear. The world could never know how sinful and dirty I really felt inside. No matter how much I achieved, the void was never filled. The voice of unworthiness was so loud. Just like in childhood, I was afraid of truly being seen. But the soul whispers deep inside were nudging me in a new direction.

It all came to a head in 2012. I experienced a massive layoff after nearly a decade with Hewlett-Packard. The layoff was a blessing in disguise, allowing me to question:

Who Am I? What do I really want?

While watching an episode of *Oprah*, in which she and her producer attended the event "Unleash the Power Within," Oprah engaged in deep spiritual discussions with Tony Robbins, experienced tremendous breakthroughs, and even walked on fire! I knew that was where I needed to be.

After my fire walk, I joined Tony's Platinum Partnership and traveled the world, learning from him and an elite group of enlightened entrepreneurs. This new world of thought I was exposed to led me deeper into my journey of personal development and healing.

Books like Napoleon Hill's *Think and Grow Rich*, Bruce Wilkinson's *The Dream Giver* and *The Prayer of Jabez*, Don Miguel Ruiz's *The Four Agreements*, Paolo Coelho's *The Alchemist*, and George Samuel Clason's *The Richest Man in Babylon* planted seeds in my consciousness for a new way of thinking.

There is a place beyond fear and dogma, a place of faith in oneself and our ability to be whatever we want to be in this life. What we truly are, are spiritual beings having a human experience.

Over time, I began to realize that the little girl I was, who laid on the warm concrete searching for truth in the cloudy sky, was embarking on the greatest journey of her life. She knew something I now know: that we don't need an intermediary to convene with God when God is in us All. It's not that God's word is flawed; it's often man's interpretation of God's word that is flawed.

The Hawaiian proverb *'A'ohe pau ka 'ike i ka hālau ho'okahi* here translates as "All knowledge is not taught in the same school." This means no person, philosophy, or organization has all the answers. One can learn from a multitude of sources.

I've had the privilege of being exposed to many great teachers, philosophies, and healing modalities, such as neuro-linguistic programming (NLP) and Ayahuasca (the sacred plant medicine of the Amazon rainforest), that have transformed my life for the better. I've studied Theosophy, Kabbalah, Buddhism, Hermetic Principles, Universal Laws, and more. These spiritual teachings expanded my consciousness and understanding of the Divine in so many ways!

I did choose this path. This Life. These circumstances. I gained so much from my upbringing as a Jehovah's Witness. Although I am no longer officially a part of that organization, there are jewels I will always cherish. Giving talks at congregation meetings honed my speaking skills, while the door-to-door ministry taught me to overcome objections and persevere. Despite facing rejection, I gained the courage to speak to anyone about my beliefs.

My parents even bestowed upon me the gift of my name. Havilah, from Genesis 2:11, *a land of gold in the garden of Eden.* How prophetic that my life's mission is to discover the gold that is within me and help others to uncover and amplify their own.

Together, humanity can accomplish great things. I walked on fire! And most importantly, learned how to walk through the fires of life.

LIVING BEYOND THE BOX

Even freedom has a cost. There are friends and family who no longer acknowledge my existence because I do not fit in their box. But the price of losing everything was worth it because I gained myself.

There are no longer any parts of me that are hidden. The totality of who I am is whole and worthy of being fully expressed in the world. I learned to love and accept myself, my thoughts, my curiosity, and my spirituality.

No circumstance or experience in life can confine or define us unless we allow it to.

Today, I get to be who I love while doing what I love. As an executive producer, award-winning actress, and three-time number one best-selling author, I have been featured on NBC, ABC, CBS, FOX, the *Huffington Post,* and more as well as sharing powerful stories on network television, in films, books, and with audiences through the spoken word. My accomplishments are no longer a mask I wear to hide, but the fuel that feeds my soul and helps me fulfill my purpose of being a catalyst for positive change in over 2 billion people's lives.

We are here on this Earth for a brief moment in relation to our true, infinite, divine nature. May we all realize that we are loved, have a purpose, and are powerful beyond measure.

Whatever you think you are . . . you are so much more. You are Proof Of What's Possible. And don't you ever forget it!

"I AM PROOF OF WHAT'S POSSIBLE."
By Havilah Malone

HAVILAH MALONE BIOGRAPHY

Havilah Malone, founder of Proof of What's Possible, is a multi-talented artist and entrepreneur on a mission to be a catalyst for positive change in over 2 billion people's lives. The three-time best-selling author, award-winning actress, spoken word artist, and executive producer inspires and equips leaders to unlock their intuitive genius and confidently communicate their value. Havilah graduated from the University of New Orleans at the age of nineteen with two degrees. By age twenty-one, she was managing a $160 million technology division for Hewlett-Packard while also serving as their television spokesperson on QVC and HSN. The former Ms. Louisiana Universal is known for her roles in HBO's *Barry*, *NCIS: New Orleans*, and numerous national TV campaigns, including four Super Bowl commercials.

Ms. Malone is a recipient of the 2025 Trailblazer of the Year Award for Acting, the 2024 Gold Telly Award, the Volunteer Service Award Gold Medal from the President of the United States, and the Network of Outstanding Women (NOW) 2023 "Artist of Year" Award. Havilah holds several professional accreditations, including master certified practitioner of NLP (neuro-linguistic programming), Silva Method, and certified instructor for the Napoleon Hill Foundation. Havilah's number one best-selling books include: *Rewriting a New History: A Spiritual Path to Audacious Authenticity and Healing*; *Think and Grow Rich* children's classic, *The Amazing Adventures of Oliver Young Napoleon Hill*, written in collaboration with the Napoleon Hill Foundation; and *How to Become a Publicity Magnet: In Any Market via TV, Radio, and Print*. Her NEW spoken word album, *Proof of What's Possible*, is available now on all music streaming platforms! For media inquiries, speaking engagements, or bookings visit:

Website: www.HavilahMalone.com
Follow on Social: IG @HavilahMalone, FB @HavilahMalone2, #BeProofOfWhatsPossible

CHAPTER 8

WALKING THROUGH THE FIRE: A JOURNEY OF FAITH, RESILIENCE, AND PURPOSE

"Faith is not about having all the answers before moving forward. Faith is moving forward despite not having all the answers."

By Angela Webb

In "Walking Through The Fire," Angela Webb courageously recounts her deeply personal journey through pain, loss, and profound transformation. As a victim advocate, Angela spent years helping others navigate their darkest moments, but a life-altering car accident shattered her world, leaving her physically and emotionally broken. Yet, in the midst of her struggles, a new calling emerged—one that drove her to prevent trauma before it began, particularly for young people.

This heartfelt memoir is a story of survival and a profound testament to the power of trusting in God's timing, embracing the unknown, and walking through life's valleys with unwavering faith. Angela's message is clear: no matter the depth of the struggle, we are never alone, and through it all, we are being prepared for something greater than we can imagine.

WALKING THROUGH THE FIRE: A JOURNEY OF FAITH, RESILIENCE, AND PURPOSE

There are moments in life when everything feels like it's falling apart. The setbacks, the disappointments, the unanswered prayers—can make even the strongest person question whether the vision placed on their heart was ever real. I know this feeling intimately. My journey wasn't just about surviving hardship; it was about learning to walk through the fire and come out refined. Faith was not my backup plan—it was my only plan. And when the world told me to quit, to take the safe route, I chose to believe in the unseen. I chose resilience.

THE CALL THAT WASN'T A CONFERENCE CALL

Victim advocacy had always been more than just work—it was a calling. For over a decade, I served as a crisis responder, stepping into the aftermath of tragedy and guiding individuals through some of the darkest moments of their lives. I became an expert in grief, witnessing firsthand how a single moment could alter the course of someone's future. But one particular event involving youth changed everything.

I remember the weight of that moment—the heartbreaking reality of a young life forever changed by one impulsive decision. It was no longer just about responding to trauma; my heart shifted toward preventing it. I felt an undeniable pull to reach young people before life-altering decisions were made—before they found themselves on the other side of an irreversible moment.

That realization shook me. It became clear that while crisis response was necessary, it wasn't enough. I couldn't just stand on the sidelines, showing up after the damage had already been done. I wanted to intervene before the trauma, before the mistakes, before the regrets. I knew this was my purpose.

But what I didn't know was that stepping into this calling would require walking through my own fire first. I never imagined that prevention work could become a full-time career—until life threw me into a storm I never saw coming.

A series of traumatic life events, followed by a devastating rollover crash, left me broken. The physical pain was one thing, but the emotional weight of it all felt unbearable. The irony wasn't lost on me—I had spent years helping others navigate their darkest moments, and now I was living in my own. My world had been turned upside down, and every part of me wanted to retreat into safety, to let go of the vision I had once held so clearly.

When I received a financial settlement, my doctors and attorneys advised me to use it for surgery to restore what had been damaged and lost. It seemed like the logical choice. After all, what was more important than restoring my own body? But deep down, I knew God had a different plan. That money wasn't meant to fix my back, neck, or eye; it was meant to give vision to something greater. That was when I faced my next test of faith.

Before my crash, I had already endured a deep personal struggle—infertility. I had always dreamed of a large family, something I cherished growing up. I had imagined a house full of children, laughter echoing through the halls, siblings growing up side by side. After years of trying and undergoing a series of IVF treatments,

I finally became pregnant. It was a miracle in itself, as I had no viable embryos left after insemination. I knew in my heart that my child was meant to be. But with that gift came the realization that I would never be able to have more children. The loss of that dream weighed on me in ways I couldn't put into words.

Perhaps that was why my heart was so drawn to working with youth. They became the children I couldn't have, the young lives I could still pour into. Maybe God wasn't withholding—maybe He was redirecting. It was as if He was showing me: *This is where your impact will be. This is where your purpose lies.* I wasn't meant to raise a household full of children, but I was meant to help shape and protect a generation. And once I fully embraced that, my mission became even clearer.

With the settlement from the car accident, I started a nonprofit to reach youth through prevention education. It felt like everything was finally aligning—but then the floor was ripped out from under me. Contracts were withheld. Promises of funding fell through. One setback after another threatened everything I had built.

This is where most people would have walked away. And trust me, I considered it. The self-doubt, the fear, the crushing weight of failure—it was real. The sleepless nights, wondering how I would keep things afloat, were overwhelming. I questioned whether I had misunderstood my calling, whether I had been too ambitious, whether I had risked too much.

But faith is not about having all the answers before moving forward. Faith is moving forward despite not having all the answers. I reminded myself that this calling was never a conference call. God didn't give this vision to everyone—He gave it to me. Not everyone would understand it, and that was okay. It wasn't meant for them. It was meant for me.

So, I pressed on. I chose to trust that if God had brought me this far, He would not leave me stranded. And as I look back now, I see how every setback, every challenge, and every moment of uncertainty was actually setting me up for something greater. Because when God gives you a vision, He also gives you everything you need to see it through—even when the road is anything but clear.

THE RIGHT VOICE MATTERS

Through all of this, I learned another critical lesson: be careful who you share your heart with. Not everyone deserves access to your dreams. Some people will see your vision and cheer you on, while others will look at you with skepticism, questioning why you would risk so much on something so uncertain. Their words might sound logical, even well-intentioned, but doubt disguised as wisdom is still doubt.

Doubters will tell you to quit, to pack up, to be "realistic." They will remind you of the risks, the what-ifs, and the countless reasons why something won't work. And if you're not careful, you'll start to believe them. You'll shrink your dreams down to fit within their limited understanding. You'll abandon the very thing God placed on your heart because someone who was never meant to see the vision convinced you it wasn't possible.

But faith-driven people? They are different. They may not fully understand your calling, but they trust the God who called you. They will encourage the walk, even when they don't have all the answers themselves. They won't let fear dictate the conversation. Instead, they will remind you that the same God who gave you the vision also gave you the strength to carry it out.

I've come to understand that the voices we allow in our lives will either fuel our faith or feed our fear. That's why choosing who you surround yourself with is just as important as the vision itself. Faith isn't about having all the answers—it's about believing in what you cannot yet see. And in those moments when doubt creeps in, you need people who will remind you of what God has already spoken over your life, not those who will question whether you heard Him correctly.

God is too big to be limited by human logic. The moment we can fully wrap our brains around Him is the moment we've made Him too small. If He has placed a vision on your heart, He has also given you everything you need to see it through—even if the path is riddled with obstacles. Not everyone will see what you see, and that's okay. Your vision wasn't meant for them; it was meant for you. And the voices you choose to listen to will determine whether you keep walking in faith or stay stuck in fear.

WALKING THROUGH, NOT CAMPING OUT

Psalm 23 has always been my anchor, but one part of the scripture speaks to me the most: "Though I walk through the valley of the shadow of death . . ." The key words? *Walk through*. Not stop. Not camp out. Not run back. Walk through.

There is something powerful about the action of moving forward, even when everything around you is telling you to give up. Valleys are not meant to be permanent places; they are seasons we must pass through. Yet, in our weakest moments, when the darkness feels unbearable, the temptation to stop and stay put is overwhelming.

I know this feeling well. There were many times I wanted to turn back. When I relocated from Northern California to Southern California, I stepped out in faith, believing that promised contracts were on the way. I uprooted my life with expectation and purpose, only to be met with disappointment. The funding that had been assured never fully materialized. I received only four months of pay for a twelve-month contract. Panic and doubt set in—had I made a mistake? Had I misheard God?

Then, six months later came COVID-19; a storm I never saw coming. Everything we had built relied on in-person programs. School assemblies, community presentations, hands-on education—everything shut down overnight. In an instant, the foundation I had worked tirelessly to build seemed to crumble. The easy choice would have been to let the business die and walk away, to return to crisis response or real estate, where stability was more certain. Relying on myself instead of God would have been the safe route.

But something inside me wouldn't let me quit. I kept hearing those words: *walk through*. Not around. Not backward. Through. So, I pivoted. I restructured everything. I created two additional formats for our programs—virtual presentations and self-paced digital courses—to ensure that our contracts and grants remained intact.

There were no guarantees, just faith and determination. Every step forward felt like walking on shifting ground, but I refused to stop moving. Keeping my staff employed during that time of turmoil and uncertainty became my priority. There were nights I stayed awake, staring at the ceiling, wondering how we would make it to the next month. But God always provided. Every need was met. Every challenge found a solution.

What started as a survival strategy turned into a lasting transformation. Even now, years later, our programs still offer those three formats, reaching more youth than ever before. The hardship forced innovation. The crisis led to expansion. It was never the way I had planned, but it was exactly the way God had already seen it.

Looking back, I realize that valleys don't just test us—they prepare us. The struggle of walking through is what strengthens our faith. When we refuse to camp out in our fear, our failures, or our setbacks, we step into something greater. Because victory isn't found in avoiding the valley. It's found in walking through it.

THE COST OF GROWTH: A LEAP OF FAITH

After three years of remarkable growth, I was faced with another defining moment—one that would test my faith, resilience, and willingness to embrace uncertainty. The success of our programs was undeniable. The data showed it, the testimonials reinforced it, and the demand for expansion was evident. Schools were reaching out, asking for more. Youth were engaging in ways we had never seen before. The impact was real, and the momentum was undeniable.

But not everyone saw what I saw. My business partner wanted to keep things the same—comfortable, predictable, and safe. Expansion meant risk. It meant stepping outside of what was already working and into uncharted territory. To me, it was the only way forward, but to them, it was unnecessary. The vision that had once united us was no longer aligned.

I wrestled with the decision for months. Letting go of that partnership wasn't just a business move; it was a painful separation from someone who had been part of the journey. I questioned everything—was I making a mistake? Was I letting ambition cloud my judgment? But deep down, I knew staying still wasn't an option. Stagnation wasn't an option.

The choice to part ways came with a cost far greater than I had anticipated. In order to sustain my vision and keep my programs moving forward, I had to make a sacrifice that few people understood—I had to forgo my salary for an entire year just to keep my employees on staff. Every logical part of me screamed that it was reckless, that I had responsibilities, that I was risking too much. Fear crept in. How would I survive? How would I take care of my child? What if I was wrong? What if all of this crumbled beneath me, and I was left with nothing?

But in those moments of doubt, I returned to one unshakable truth: the dream was bigger than the fear. And so, I pressed on.

That year of sacrifice stretched me in ways I never could have imagined. There were months when the numbers didn't add up, when I had no idea how I was going to make it to the next paycheck, when I had to rely on faith alone to push forward. I had to lean on God in ways I never had before, trusting that if He had brought me this far, He wouldn't let me fall now.

And then, the impossible happened. That year of sacrifice led to exponential growth—quadrupling our contracts, tripling our programs, and expanding our impact from 5,000 youth to over 100,000 in a single year. Opportunities that I never even pursued came knocking at my door. Partnerships that had once seemed out of reach became a reality. The vision was no longer just a dream—it was happening. The calling was real. The purpose was real. And through it all, God was faithful.

Looking back, I realize that growth will always require sacrifice. Sometimes, it means letting go of comfort. Sometimes, it means walking away from what's familiar. And sometimes, it means betting on a vision that no one else can see but you. But when God plants a vision in your heart, He will always make a way—even when the path seems impossible.

GOD'S FAITHFULNESS AND THE DESIRES OF MY HEART

God's goodness and faithfulness didn't stop there—He fulfilled another promise. Psalm 37:4 (NIV) says, "Delight yourself in the Lord, and He will give you the desires of your heart."

For years, I had grieved the loss of my dream of a large family, carrying both gratitude and sorrow in my heart. I cherished every single second with my daughter, knowing she was my greatest blessing, yet there was an unspoken ache for the family I had always envisioned.

In the midst of pouring into the lives of thousands of youths, God was shaping something beyond what I could see. He was preparing something greater—something that would heal parts of me I didn't even realize still needed healing.

And then, out of nowhere, He brought an incredible man into my life. A man whose heart mirrored mine, whose humor was infectious, and whose strength was unwavering. He had walked through his own valleys yet stood unwavering in faith and integrity. He saw me—not just the strong, independent woman I had become, but the woman who had endured loss, fought battles in silence, and still chose to love deeply.

With him, I found not just love but the family I had longed for: four stepchildren who welcomed me as their *bonus mom* and four grandchildren whose laughter filled every space of our home. A house that wasn't just full, but whole—overflowing with love, loyalty, and joy in the purest, most authentic form.

God's plan was never to replace what I had lost but to fulfill a promise in a way I could never have imagined. He knew the desires of my heart long before I even spoke them. He knew the family I longed for, the connection I craved, and the love that would bring a new kind of completeness. And He delivered—right on time, in His perfect way.

I had spent so many years believing that my dream of a big family had slipped away, only to realize that God was never withholding—He was preparing. And as I stand in the midst of this beautiful, unexpected blessing, I am reminded once again that His faithfulness is unwavering. His promises never fail. And when we trust Him fully, even in our seasons of waiting, He delivers not just what we asked for—but something infinitely greater.

A MESSAGE TO THE WOMAN WALKING THROUGH THE FIRE

To the woman reading this who feels like the weight of the world is pressing down on her—who feels like giving up because everything is falling apart—I want you to know this: you were never meant to stay in the valley.

You may feel like this season will never end; that the pain is too heavy, the disappointment too deep, the obstacles too many. You may be standing at the edge of a decision—do you keep fighting or do you let go? Do you press on or do you shrink back?

I've been there. I know the exhaustion of carrying dreams that feel impossible, of watching doors slam shut, of wondering if God has forgotten you. But hear me—you were not called to camp out in your struggle. You were called to walk through it.

The fire you're facing right now may feel like it's meant to consume you, but I promise you—it's refining you. It's strengthening you. It's shaping you into the woman you were always meant to be. The hardest seasons in our lives are not detours; they are the very road God is using to prepare us for what's next.

I know how easy it is to let fear and doubt whisper lies into your heart: *You're not strong enough. You're not capable. You'll never make it through this.* But let me remind you of the truth—fear is a liar. Doubt is a thief. And the voices that try to convince you to quit are not speaking from faith; they are speaking from their own limitations.

Keep walking. Keep believing. Keep holding on to the vision that God placed inside of you. And as I stand on the other side of my own fire, I can tell you this with certainty: resilience is a choice, and faith is the foundation that makes it possible.

Resilience isn't just about surviving—it's about thriving. It's about choosing to believe in what you cannot yet see, choosing to trust that God's plan is bigger than your current struggle, choosing to take one more step even when everything in you wants to stop. And if there is one thing I pray over you, it's this—we don't know how or when our stories will end, but may it never read, "she gave up."

Not you. Not today. Not ever.

Keep walking. Your breakthrough is coming.
"I AM RESILIENT. I AM LOVED."
By Angela Webb

ANGELA WEBB BIOGRAPHY

Angela Webb is an internationally recognized crisis intervention specialist, youth advocate, and empowerment leader dedicated to saving lives and transforming communities. As the founder and CEO of Arrive Alive California (AAC), she has impacted over a quarter-million individuals, equipping them with life-saving knowledge surrounding prevention and well-being.

Her commitment to crisis response began as a volunteer trauma responder, earning her the President's Volunteer Service Award in 2011. Angela's expertise has been featured on nationally syndicated TV, major news networks, and top publications, including *Forbes, CEO Weekly, USA Wire, Yahoo News, News Nation*, and the *Dr. Phil Show*. Ranked among the Top 100 Women Entrepreneurs, Global Women Magazine, she is also a sought-after motivational speaker, inspiring audiences with messages of resilience, transformation, and mental mastery.

At the heart of her work is a lifelong commitment to serving others and creating lasting change.

CONNECT WITH ANGELA:

Follow on Socials: IG and FB @iamAngelaWebb

CHAPTER 9

GOD'S GIFTS IN DESPERATION

"To sparkle from the inside out, we must drink from the fountain of healing and inner work!"

By Allison Eve Doss

In "God's Gifts in Desperation," Allison Doss courageously opens her heart to share the raw and transformative story of her journey from self-destruction to self-liberation. Battling addiction, trauma, and broken relationships, Allison finds herself at rock bottom—only to discover that her deepest pain would lead to the most profound healing. Through a powerful moment of divine intervention, she learns to release control, surrender her expectations, and embrace the grace of vulnerability.

This heartfelt memoir is not just a tale of survival but of rediscovery—where faith, forgiveness, and the gift of inner peace guide her toward a new purpose. In the end, Allison realizes that her journey, though fraught with hardship, has empowered her to serve others and share the light she's found, helping others find their way to freedom and spiritual growth.

* See Disclaimer 1

GOD'S GIFTS IN DESPERATION

It all happened so fast! It's as if I had awakened one morning from falling asleep watching a movie. Only this feature film had been the last forty-five years of my life! It was all a blur. I felt like the main character in a drama-filled story written by someone else.

Was this the midlife crisis I used to hear my parents talk about—the one where the neighbor abruptly quit his job, left his wife, and got a Corvette? Was this the inevitable identity crisis that opened its door and welcomed everyone in as they reached their midterm of existence? I sat in confusion and dismay as I grasped for meaning and comfort in my identity and purpose.

I had constantly rolled through life with such oblivion to what would be next, and I was definitely never prepared to be a woman in her late forties with no savings, no husband, and no vision for a bright and promising future. It made sense, though, because after graduating from high school, when all my classmates eagerly applied to colleges, I hastily planned my escape from my small-town, rural cage.

Everybody knew everybody! I couldn't get away with anything. I was never one to take the path of least resistance, and minding rules was not on my list of top priorities. My dad was controlling and ruled the house with a dominating iron fist. His need to control and my need to not be controlled clashed for years under the same roof. Even when I was out of the house, anything that I did was viewed by the judging eyes of everyone in town. Mom and Dad would get the call, and I was grounded again! Riding around town in a friend's car, skipping school, smoking a cigarette behind the town store—no matter what it was, I was forever found out!

I could not wait to leave that town when I graduated from high school because I no longer wanted to be held accountable by anyone. I wanted to explore the world without a single soul telling me how or when to do it.

It didn't take long to be devoured by 'all that glittered' in the big city of Washington, D.C. Seeking money and attention from men was a disastrous yet perfect recipe for me in the underground and very popular scene of stripping, sex, and drugs. I spent so many years in an altered state of mind and redefining my moral compass that I plummeted into a spiral that was a formidable adversary.

The years cycloned around me with such veracity that the next fifteen years were an EF5 tornado that included the birth of two boys—whom I lost physical custody of—many jail visits, traumatic sexual encounters, loss of esteem, and a life full of guilt, shame, drug-filled rage, and homelessness.

The dust began to settle when I found myself, at the age of forty, peeling myself off the dirty floor of a run-down drug house known as a trap house on a hot July fourth South Florida day. I had just been attacked by another drug addict who sliced my face in a fury to regain her territory in the trap. As terrifying, unwelcome, and violent as that moment was, I now know that I would not have had that moment of clarity to begin to reclaim my life had I not been stopped dead in my tracks in such a jarring way. I will forever refer to this moment as God's gift in desperation.

Are there times in your life that you now look back on and, although it was so painful, if it weren't for that precise moment, things wouldn't be how they are now?

I have so many patterns of proof that things are happening for a reason, although we don't know it at the time or realize the many blessings on the other side of all that we endure.

Shortly after I began the slow road to recovery, I met the man who would become my husband. I never thought that I could be the marrying type! Men had always been expendable to me, and with the self-willed riot I had always been, that made perfect sense. But I was changing for the better. My attachment to this man was a beautiful distraction from who I had been, the damage I'd caused with my children, and the answer to redefining who I was.

I was so convinced that the new me was on the right track that I failed at recognizing the glowing red flags as they feverishly slapped in the wind and directly into my face. But I was so used to the chaos inside my body that I nestled in and made myself at home. After all, I had never had any boundaries nor the ability to recognize that my boundaries were being crossed, so it was onward, soldier!

During this time, I was making a slight effort to communicate with my children, but I was so hell-bent on meeting my partner's needs that, sadly, my children's needs came last.

Have you been guilty of this, Mom?

This is a cycle that left me—and will leave you—in a pit of shame and guilt. It's like quicksand that continually pulls you back down to the reality that your choices are stabbing your children in the back.

For years, I allowed my self-esteem and value to be dictated by the response and behavior I received from a man I had made my higher power. God will always have the most clever ways to bring us back down to size. I didn't think anything could top the humble pie of having my face sliced, but I was mistaken.

Just one year into my marriage, my husband confessed to me that he believed he was transgender. Yes, transgender.

The man I had been pouring myself into for the previous five years split my new identity of 'wifey' entirely in two. I felt this crack deep within my soul, and my body began to tremble from the inside out. But I was so used to maneuvering in such a way that I knew I could figure out how to put this cat back in the bag, keep it all moving, and keep it all together.

After all, I had sacrificed my boundaries and closer relationships with my children on a mission to please my man. He owed it to me not to do anything to destroy the life we had and the future I saw for us! I had put up with so much over the years. The transgender confession hadn't just come out of nowhere. There had been so many signs along the way—the manicured nails, the women's underwear, the submissive sexual requests. And though the static in my body loudly rejected these things, my label as "wife" kept me clinging to the fantasy of how our life together could be and should be.

The transgender confession sliced through my delusion, just as that glass had sliced my face a few short years before. I had no choice but to gather the facts of what really was and begin to sift through the ashes of what I had created in my mind. The reality was that my husband was on a journey where I felt no longer welcomed.

My heart was broken. I could not understand how there was anything more important to my husband than me.

Have you ever felt that way? Have you ever felt so small, devalued, unseen, and unheard by someone who vowed to do the opposite?

The onslaught on my self-worth was an armed force that stormed my existence every morning and tactically removed my value throughout the day. During this time, my doubt and confusion blinded me to the possibility of anything good coming out of this situation. But true to form, God always has other plans! And oh, such beautiful plans they are.

Shortly after leaving my husband, I was granted the gift of having my oldest son move in with me. This blessing could only have resulted from my living alone with an extra bedroom to welcome my son when he came knocking. Having the opportunity to love my son, whom I had selfishly deserted so many years ago, was the beginning of a healing that only God could gift-wrap.

There were many truths that I was forced to contend with after leaving my husband, heartbroken and attempting to move on with my life.

EXPECTATION

For a lifetime, I had lived in the facade that I had the power to control the people around me, and when it came to the men in my life, I had basically been successful! I had a toolbox for controlling others. When my husband came out as transgender, I reached into that box and behold! The curtain opened, and the maestro began leading the artistic direction of my masterful manipulation.

All of these tools I had used in the past—and with great success. The screaming would be center front, using the most intimidating tone I could muster. The shame-filled rhetoric that spewed from my forked tongue was the second act. I can never take back the horrible things I said—only apologize and offer living amends not to hurt others with words.

The third was withholding sex. Many of us do this to get what we want from our partners. I will never use my body again as leverage or in an attempt to manipulate. When the screaming, shaming, and holding my body hostage failed to win the war, I threatened to leave. And when my husband's transition didn't stall, I left.

I just knew that one of my 'controlling others' tools would force my husband into submission. I expected it! Are you currently using any of these tools with the expectation that your partner will one day drop to a bent knee and wave the white flag? Do not be confused. All of these tactics are selfish, self-seeking, and manipulative. Expecting our loved ones to submit to our vision of how they should act or be will only leave you with resentment.

RESENTMENT

Resentment is the thief of peace. A wise man once claimed that resentment is like drinking poison and expecting your enemy to die. The enemy here is our loved one that we want to control. Of course, we don't want them to die, but we want them to submit! "Do as I say, so I'll be okay!"

The resentment that I carried toward my husband's transition was killing me. I was unable to accept it, and I was unable to continue the marriage. I resented him so greatly for not choosing me, as my husband had vowed to do at our beach wedding the year prior. How was I going to forgive him for changing? How would I forgive myself for being unable to be with the new person? It was all such a mess.

Radical acceptance was necessary, but it evaded me. How was I supposed to just let go of the life we had, the life we wanted, the life I expected? It became abundantly clear that my human power—no one's human power—would be able to alleviate my resentments and perhaps your resentments.

We must turn it all over to an all-powerful God of our understanding.

But how?

PRAYER

Amid pain, confusion, and anger, begging God to take it all away was my Hail Mary. I had never been one to relinquish control, but my ways were failing me, and I was desperate. What a beautiful safety net we have when all else seems to fail.

I don't know about you, but my prayers during that time were more of pleading and begging. At first, I begged God to bring my husband back to me. If only that prayer could be answered, I would be relieved of my broken heart. I needed relief, and I expected God to provide.

A friend and mentor suggested that I begin focusing my prayer on my husband. She said God was probably tired of my self-pity and would appreciate it if I prayed for others. That sounded horrendous to me then, but I gave it a shot. Over the next few weeks, I prayed for my husband—his pain, his journey. I even asked God to remove my selfish motives and show me the way through this experience, which both of us were, in fact, struggling with.

Have you ever done that? Have you ever prayed for the person who was breaking your heart? Have you ever asked God to care for the person you resent the most?

It changes everything.

When you remove yourself from being the director, the producer, and the actor in your film of life, God moves in and does what only God can. Resentment and expectation are our way of holding on to control of the outcome of all of our relationships. Allowing God to be the ultimate Director of your life is the defining key to freedom from attachment to every outcome in your life.

Thank God!

SURRENDER

I relinquished all control. I let go of my need to control my husband, his path, and his transition. That was not easy. On my bent knee, I asked God to take the wheel every day! I proclaimed my gratitude for the beautiful life I had been given and continued to ask God to remove my expectations of others, my need to control and fix everyone, and my desire to be the director.

Surrender takes action! Throughout the day, as we all do, I jumped back into the director's chair, tying the puppet strings to the people at work, my adult child, and my friends. *If only they would act as I think they should, all would be well.* Over and over, every day, these delusional thoughts would hijack my brain. I would feel tense and go into 'control it all' mode.

But armed with the facts that only God is in control and absolutely no one needs my input to live their lives, I can take a deep breath, ask God to remove those intrusive thoughts and free myself from the expectations that heavy resentment would have likely followed.

Living a life free of trying to control the people you love and being able to meet them where they're at is the answer to your freedom and your peace. God is either everything or God is nothing. It is up to you to choose.

Do you choose freedom from self? Or do you choose to cling to the delusion that you are all-powerful, here to insert your will and power onto the ones you hold so dear to your heart?

I choose freedom.

Surrender yourself, and you will feel free.

SERVICE

So, why am I writing all of this? Why am I sharing the struggle of my most intimate moments with the reader of this book? One word: service. The lessons I've learned from this bumpy road of life have profoundly affected my confidence. The wisdom resulting from such brave introspection of self truly makes a woman sparkle.

Exposing the light within is only possible by removing the damning character defects that cloud our judgment, distance us from others, and create an image of self that is simply untrue.

Carrying resentment through life because of unmet expectations were the two defective character traits that stunted my spiritual growth for far too long.

Do you relate?

Now that I have this freedom, I must share the good news!

Every breakup, addiction, or hardship you've overcome can be a survival guide for someone looking to find their way through exactly where you've been. We are responsible for being a beacon of light and sharing vulnerably with those we encounter.

I hope that my vulnerability permits you to be vulnerable. The path I've walked has given me purpose. And yours can, too! A purpose-filled life is inspired by healing from your traumas, forgiving others, letting go of control of the people around you, and, most importantly, sharing your healing journey with other women. Simply put, being of service to others is the reason we exist!

THE GLOW

There is an inarguable radiance that is emitted from a woman who is brave enough to explore her innermost self. She comes face to face with her flaws and character defects, and instead of building walls around them to protect herself from others, she bravely dismantles the armor that has thus far been needed in her life to survive.

But let me be clear. We will no longer accept only surviving in this life of ours. We will thrive! The burning embers of healing start as a small flame but eventually burn as bright as the stars in the night sky. Having cleared all of the resentment and anger that unexpectedly separate us from the God inside, we emerge as a beacon of hope to those around us.

We've been told a million times that we must drink a lot of water for our skin to be beautiful. To sparkle from the inside out, we must drink from the fountain of healing and inner work. We must always question what our relationships and our surroundings are trying to teach us about ourselves. We must always ask ourselves how we can be of service to others. And we must always trust a God of our understanding to guide and support us.

This is the work that genuinely elevates our vibration. This is a vibration that every passerby will see as YOUR inner sparkle.

I wish I could tell you that these lessons of freedom came to me one night like a comet barreling through the sky with one sole mission—to heal me. These realizations were slow to appear, and I was even slower to act upon them. God's time is simply that—God's. It is not ours to force us to be faster for our desires and needs.

I'm grateful for that now. During this time of healing, I made peace with my divorce from my husband. I have since apologized for my behavior during the earthquake of transition, and I have been forgiven for how I attempted to manipulate and control the situation.

I tried my best to be a friend, someone supportive that my ex could call and share his new life as a transwoman with, but it was like I was trying to fit a square peg into a round hole. And though I had always been known to be one to bang my head against a concrete wall until my head split open, the wise woman in me has chosen to let go.

I let go of my need to fulfill my ex's needs before mine. The journey through my divorce has been much like my journey in sobriety. All of the key components are the same—a daily, brave self-introspection about the ways and means that I expect the world to show up for me and let go of my need to control it all. I seek God in good times and bad.

My relationships with my children are the silver lining in this journey of healing and sobriety. No longer existing in shame and guilt for the pain that I've caused is something I wish for every mom. Viewing my children as God's children and not my own has allowed me to release the reins of controlling their path and force-feeding them to live life the way that I think they should.

What a relief!

These blessings and gifts were born out of the most desperate moments of my life thus far. What a promise to know that God still has gifts for these moments, too!

Where are you now in this life you have been given? Are you where I was? Are you sitting in confusion, wondering how it all happened so fast? How did I get here? Where do I go from here? Are you in the midlife crisis that was crippling me, too?

I'm here to tell you that we aren't going to look in the rearview mirror anymore. Instead, we will be forward-facing with a foot on the gas, and I'll tell you—the view looks good from here. Are you ready to change your mindset and shift your energy?

It all starts with acknowledging where we expect people to be or who we think they should be. A magical moment ignites the soul when you are gifted with the clarity that all your resentments are simply your unmet expectations of how you believe the world should show up for you.

I have relieved myself of my expectations of how I think things should be or how people should act by accepting things exactly as they are and meeting them where they're at—without imposing my delusional reality upon them. And with that, I can rest knowing that nothing in God's plan is by mistake. God is in control.

Surrender yourself to a God of your understanding. Let God help you live a life with the ultimate freedom of releasing your attachment to the outcome of the world you so desperately try to control. Let it go, girl!

And when the weight of your past—the traumas, heartbreaks, and unmet expectations—begins to lift, don't forget to share your success and the things you have learned with the women you meet along the way who also yearn to be free.

Surrender. Service. Sparkle.
"I AM"
By Allison Eve Doss

ALLISON EVE DOSS BIOGRAPHY

Allison Doss is a three-time best-selling author of *The Unbossing*, which earned the prestigious International Impact Award in 2024. A dynamic speaker, she has taken the stage at the Networking of Outstanding Women (NOW) Honors, Speaker Hearts, and the International Impact Awards. She has been featured on numerous podcasts worldwide.

Allison's journey is a testament to the power of resilience, transformation, and self-discovery. Once caught in the grip of addiction and homelessness, she made the courageous choice to reclaim her life, embracing sobriety and personal growth. Just as she began to rebuild, an unexpected confession from her husband challenged her strength once more. She prioritized her happiness with unwavering self-respect, forging a path that honors her true self.

Now, as a transformational speaker, coach, and author, Allison empowers others to rise above their own challenges, rewrite their stories, and step into their full potential.

CONNECT WITH ALLISON:

Website: www.allisondoss.com
Follow on Social: IG @therealbossdoss

CHAPTER 10

RADIATE YOUR INNER SPARKLE: THE SACRED ART OF SELF-NURTURING

**"We have the power to transform our lives
one nurturing choice at a time."**

By Kelley Grimes MSW

*"Radiate Your Inner Sparkle: The Sacred Art of Self-Nurturing" invites
you to embark on a deeply personal and transformative journey toward
healing, strength, and empowerment. In this heartfelt chapter, Kelley
Grimes opens her heart to share the trials and triumphs of her life—
raising two daughters through health challenges; confronting her own
struggles with grief, fear, and burnout; and discovering the profound
healing power of self-nurturing.*

*Kelley's journey is a beautiful testament to the strength and light we
all carry within, reminding us that by embracing joy and compassion for
ourselves, we can not only heal but also radiate our inner sparkle to the world
around us. This chapter is an invitation to remember that we are worthy
of love, care, and the power to live with deeper meaning and connection.*

RADIATE YOUR INNER SPARKLE: THE SACRED ART OF SELF-NURTURING

When I applied for graduate school to help women cultivate resilience, strength, and self-love, I could have never imagined the challenges life would throw my way, testing my resilience and strength. In my admissions essay, I wrote about my dream of starting a multi-disciplinary women's center where women could come together to empower and nurture themselves. Having survived an abusive relationship as a teen, I was passionate about women's empowerment. In my essay, I highlighted the importance of self-nurturing and how I yearned to make the world a more just, loving, and compassionate place.

While in my second year of graduate school, I became unexpectedly pregnant with my daughter, Fiona. I was so proud of myself for completing the program while pregnant and in a constant state of nausea. After graduation, I was thrilled to be hired by the Boulder County Health Department to work with pregnant women with substance abuse challenges. Working with pregnant women while pregnant was truly magical and made creating relationships and building trust easy.

I loved supporting my clients through their pregnancies with counseling, support groups, and case management, and even during their labor and delivery if they wanted me to be there. It was my dream job, and I loved every minute of nurturing, supporting, and encouraging these inspiring women to nurture themselves and their inner sparkle at this life-changing time of their lives.

The following year, my husband received an opportunity for us to move to California. Although being closer to my family was a blessing, leaving Colorado, my husband's family, and our dear friends was difficult.

My husband's new job was demanding, and he often worked twelve-hour days, leaving little time for us as a family. I stayed home full-time with Fiona as we explored our new town, made new friends, and regularly visited the park, beach, and library.

A year later, my husband switched jobs, and I returned to work as a counselor at a domestic violence program. Fiona started attending preschool, and we moved down the coast to be closer to my family. We were settling into our new life beautifully, unaware that our lives were about to change forever.

Then, one day, during naptime at preschool, Fiona started having a seizure, and the staff did not understand what was happening. They called my husband to pick her up. When he arrived, he knew something was terribly wrong and took her directly to the hospital.

I will never forget the terror I experienced seeing her tiny, naked body seizing on the gurney. There was blood all around, a result of the unsuccessful attempts of hospital staff to place an IV into her shuddering arms and legs. The ER doctors and nurses were visibly stressed and called in the Children's Hospital ICU Transport Team. Blessedly, they placed the IV in Fiona's ankle before putting her in the ambulance.

After fifty-five minutes and trying multiple medications, they were finally able to stop the seizure, preventing her from dying. This experience left me completely traumatized. Following in our car, not allowed in the ICU ambulance, my husband and I felt helpless, confused, and terrified about what was happening.

The next three days were unimaginably stressful as we watched our sweet daughter being poked, prodded, and tested with spinal taps, CT scans, and EEGs while she cried and whimpered and begged for the boot that housed her IV to be taken off.

When she received the diagnosis of epilepsy, we were shocked and spent many hours trying to understand this neurological disorder. We were desperate to know why she had developed epilepsy and learned that, for many people, there is no known cause. Epilepsy is a condition where people experience sudden recurrent seizures caused by abnormal electrical activity in the brain. The more we researched, the more scared and devastated we became, not knowing what our precious two-year-old's future would look like.

We survived that harrowing experience and so many others during Fiona's childhood; it never got easier. Each time Fiona had a seizure, my fear and grief would resurface—sometimes crashing over me like a mighty wave and other times seeping in like a rising flood.

This fear and grief continued when, less than a year later, while I was six months pregnant with my daughter Zoey, my beloved grandmother died, and then two weeks later, my father died unexpectedly. I was overwhelmed with grief and ended up going into pre-term labor.

I was hospitalized a few times and then finally placed on bed rest for about six weeks, taking medication every three hours to prevent my baby from being born prematurely.

We were blessed that Zoey was born full term, but our family's medical challenges were far from over. For the first few years of her life, Zoey picked up every infection she was exposed to, including ear infections, croup, bronchitis, pneumonia, chicken pox, strep, scarlet fever, and staph, ending up in the hospital multiple times.

Balancing work and care for my sick daughters became increasingly challenging. At one point, Zoey was hospitalized with four infections, and the doctor feared she was immunocompromised. He suggested I quit my job and stay home with her full-time. Grappling with this decision was incredibly stressful, as I loved my work but was heartbroken that Zoey continued to suffer. Understanding that staying home with her could be the healing solution that was needed empowered me to quit my job, and Zoey began to recover and thrive.

These extraordinary experiences as a young mom taught me how to cultivate courage, strength, and resilience. Desperate to feel a sense of control when faced with my daughters' health challenges, I became an expert in nurturing others. I fine-tuned my ability to perceive my daughters' needs before they asked, looked for ways to be supportive, and developed ridiculously high expectations of myself to be constantly available and to ensure everyone's safety and well-being.

I embraced over-responsibility and caregiving like a badge of honor. There was little room in my life for me, as I spent all my waking hours focused on other people's feelings and needs. The longer I devoted my time and energy exclusively to others, the more disconnected I became with myself. In addition, I lived in a heightened state of stress, constantly prepared to manage the next crisis.

One unique challenge of epilepsy is its unpredictability, so even when Fiona was not having a seizure, I was fearful she could. Indeed, her seizures continued, and over time, we were faced with the secondary challenges of epilepsy, including medication side effects, impacts on learning, injuries from seizures, anxiety, depression, memory challenges, missed school . . . and migraines.

Fiona was eight years old when she started suffering from migraines after every seizure. The excruciating pain could last for up to five days and was accompanied by light and sound sensitivity and nausea. No medication would relieve the symptoms, although every option was tried.

And so, I would sit with her, helpless, and attempt to nurture her through the pain. A new level of grief and despair arrived with every migraine. My beloved daughter was struggling in pain, begging me to make it stop—and there was nothing I could do.

Even with my highly developed coping skills, I lived in constant fear and vigilance. When would the next seizure come? How bad would it be? I worried about her future and her ability to finish school and live independently. I never shared those fears with her. I always kept up my hopeful outlook around her, but inside, I was in crisis. Every time the phone rang, my heart skipped a beat, and every morning, I woke up wondering if I had anything else to give.

When Fiona was fourteen, she had a seizure that triggered a migraine, but this one was different. It didn't stop after five days. On day nine, I took her to the emergency room, where they were able to stop the pain with morphine—but only for half a day.

One of the medications they gave her before the morphine triggered another seizure. Over the next year, my teenage daughter and I endured more doctors, appointments, medication trials, hospitals (including the Mayo Clinic), holistic healthcare practitioners, treatments, supplements, food restrictions, and more healing approaches than I can count. At the end of it, Fiona was still in chronic pain, depressed, and hopeless.

This took me to a breaking point. One day, on a walk, I recognized how profoundly depressed I had become and how I had nothing left to give. I lacked hope that life could be different for my daughter, my family, and me. I felt the crushing weight of responsibility, despair, and hopelessness and thought that stepping in front of the next passing car would be easier than the life I was living.

I had become an expert in coping and keeping it together on the outside, but on the inside, I was drowning. I knew something had to change.

Standing on the curb, I asked myself what could stop this despair. At that moment, I heard my soul's wisdom loud and clear: *joy is the antidote to this terrible suffering*. It hit me with great clarity that to transform my life, I needed to choose joy.

The curb I was standing on symbolized this choice. Where I stepped next was up to me.

Walking home with this new insight, I experienced great freedom, as if some weight had been lifted off my heart. I felt a powerful shift in my thinking and knew a transformative process had begun.

The thought that I could choose joy had never occurred to me through all this suffering, but now that I saw this option, I could not ignore it. This new awareness energized me, and I started exploring multiple ways to cultivate joy in my life.

I began by deepening my practice of mindfulness and meditation, which was at first very challenging due to the intensity of my emotions, which I had suppressed for so long.

Each time I sat in meditation, my sadness would engulf me. Tears would stream down my face. The enormity of my grief was terrifying. I thought I would never feel anything else again if I allowed it all in. But I continued to practice, and an amazing thing happened one day. I became aware of feeling more than just grief and sadness. Finally, there was room in me for more.

With each new experience of reconnecting with myself, I began to trust my ability to be with any emotion that surfaced.

I noticed that my trust grew, and so did my self-awareness and self-compassion. I started to explore nurturing myself in new and healing ways. My meditation cushion became a bridge between my old existence of hopelessness and a new life where peace and joy could be cultivated.

There was another profound blessing in choosing joy - I learned to nurture and befriend myself! Being intentional about choosing joy encouraged me to treat myself like a dear friend with kindness and compassion.

I started acknowledging my feelings and honoring my needs, which led me to prioritize myself in my own life.

I practiced placing my hand on my heart, checking in with myself, and then asking what the most nurturing thing would be that I could do now. Through this beautiful practice, I could comfort and love myself no matter what happened. Nurturing myself allowed me to calm my nervous system, cultivate resilience, and show up more authentically in my life.

Witnessing all these benefits inspired me to embrace and grow my self-nurturing practice wholeheartedly. My inner sparkle radiated more brightly, and people noticed and commented on my peace and joy.

As my practice evolved, I learned that self-nurturing could be engaged alone and with others.

I felt nourished and rejuvenated by my self-nurturing practices of walking in nature, yoga, spending time with my family, laughing, playing games, sharing gratitude, journaling, reading uplifting books, singing, going to see live music, being creative, writing love notes, learning, being playful, and spending time with friends.

As I began to look at my life through the lens of self-nurturing, I weeded many activities out, too. I began to say yes only to activities that brought me joy and recharged me. I built with Habitat for Humanity with Fiona, joined a women's singing group, wrote regularly about self-nurturing, spent more time in nature, and traveled for the first time in years. I deepened my gratitude practice and found blessings even in the hard times.

Each experience of intentionally choosing joy made me feel more empowered, inspired, and deeply nurtured.

My ongoing feelings of being overwhelmed, grief, and depression began to recede. The profound sense of hopelessness I had experienced for years around Fiona's health challenges was transmuted into empowerment as I started to see the remarkable difference self-nurturing made in my life and for the people around me; especially Fiona. Joy and gratitude allowed me to see more possibilities for us.

I was able to develop a joy reserve so I was more resilient and did not feel as devastated when a treatment for Fiona was not successful. My capacity to hold joy and sorrow grew, and I let go of feeling I was betraying my grief when I chose joy.

As I changed, so did Fiona. Even when she was in pain, nurturing myself increased my ability to be present, compassionate, kind, and creative. I found humor in the challenges and made empowered decisions for us. My hopeful attitude, in turn, impacted Fiona, and she began to regain her sense of humor, confidence, and belief that things could be different. Both of our sparkles became brighter with this nurturing approach.

We also became deeply grounded in the understanding that Fiona was on a healing journey—a complete transformation from our lives of constant health crises, hopelessness, and despair. With this new perspective, the quality of our lives improved dramatically, and slowly but surely, things began to change.

We rooted ourselves in gratitude and focused on what was going well rather than what was not working. We looked for blessings everywhere and found them in all the helpers and healers in our lives. We transformed our scarcity mindset into an abundance mindset and were able to thrive, even though it took four more years before Fiona was mainly living pain-free.

Through this process, our family learned so much about ourselves, our resilience, our strength, and the difference embracing joy and self-nurturing can make in learning to love ourselves.

Joy has become the foundation of my self-nurturing practice. Every time I face what appears to be an insurmountable challenge, I see myself back on that curb, and I am so grateful I chose joy.

The remarkable gift of that moment of choice continues to save my life and inspires my life's work as a self-nurturing enthusiast.

Recognizing that I could choose joy, no matter how difficult the situation, and intentionally prioritizing self-nurturing have transformed my life from the inside out. My empowering decision to nurture myself has changed everything for my family and led us out of darkness into the light.

When I committed to my self-nurturing practice fifteen years ago, I dedicated myself to learning and growing my understanding of all things self-nurturing. I was so inspired by the healing ripples in my life, my daughters' lives, and the lives of my clients with whom I shared my lessons that I knew this transformational practice could help other women.

When I started researching, little was written about self-nurturing. I focused on self-nurturing instead of self-care because I believed it was more encompassing and included cultivating a relationship with ourselves, not just the activities.

I defined self-nurturing as lovingly caring for yourself by deeply nourishing, cherishing, and encouraging your growth and potential.

As I started teaching self-nurturing workshops, I would ask participants to reflect on how they nourished themselves, cherished themselves, and encouraged their growth and potential, providing them with a self-nurturing roadmap.

In these workshops, we also explored what stopped women from nurturing themselves, which universally was feeling guilty and selfish, and what consequences they experienced from not nurturing themselves. I would regularly hear people identify a long list of consequences, including illness, stress, overwhelm, exhaustion, resentment, anxiety, self-criticism, self-doubt, impatience, irritability, anger, judgment of self and others, headaches, physical pain, hopelessness, and/or feeling unfulfilled and unappreciated.

Over time, the consequences of their self-neglect became debilitating, as they had been for me. Regularly, women told me they were desperate for life to be different but did not know what to do.

I reminded them that what is liberating about self-nurturing is not about being perfect or completing another thing on their to-do lists but instead nurturing a loving and compassionate relationship with themselves. I shared my favorite self-nurturing mantras: *"Progress not perfection"* and *"Clarity is kindness,"* which helped me transform my mindset.

I invited everyone to give themselves permission to recognize what is nurturing at any moment, allow their practice to evolve accordingly, and ask for help when needed, recognizing that it may be the most nurturing and empowering choice they can make.

I became passionate about sharing my transformational self-nurturing journey and letting other women know that they can cultivate lives filled with resilience, strength, compassion, and self-love rather than living from obligation and being overwhelmed.

I highlighted the many gifts of self-nurturing, including the ongoing opportunities to learn about themselves, express their authenticity and creativity, and give from the overflow in their saucer rather than the last drops in their cup.

The old paradigm of the self-sacrificing mom is exhausting and unsustainable. Trying to live up to this unattainable ideal has made women feel like something is wrong with them and has fed their sense of unworthiness. Caring for others and neglecting themselves have left women disconnected from their feelings and needs and, ultimately, from themselves.

With self-compassion and self-love, we can transform our mindset by choosing a *both/and* approach to loving and nurturing ourselves and others. And in truth, it feels better to everyone.

A resentful, frazzled, overwhelmed giver shares all that and more with the receiver. Self-nurturing is a revolutionary choice for women to empower themselves, heal, and transform their lives, families, and communities.

By nurturing my light, I model what an empowered mother who values herself and her family looks like. I have transformed the old paradigm of the self-sacrificing mother into a woman filled with peace, joy, and meaning, radiating her inner sparkle brightly in the world.

After spending my career helping clients rebuild their belief in themselves and own their value and worth, I am so grateful to have discovered that self-nurturing is the key.

You see, the more we nurture ourselves, the more we acknowledge our value and worth. The more we acknowledge our value and worth, the more we prioritize nurturing ourselves, creating a beautiful, self-sustaining cycle.

We have the power to transform our lives, one nurturing choice at a time.

We can cultivate resilience, joy, gratitude, and wholeness with the sacred art of self-nurturing.

My daughters and I are living proof! Today, Fiona and Zoey are empowered, vibrant, healthy women. They are loving mothers of joyful children who radiate love and light everywhere. Self-nurturing is woven into the fabric of our lives, allowing us to live intentionally and with so much gratitude. Who knew during those dark times that today we would radiate our inner sparkles so brightly?

In my graduate school admissions essay over thirty years ago, I identified the importance of self-nurturing, only to find many years later that it was the key to saving my life. Knowing something intellectually does not prevent us from falling into a habit of self-neglect and caring for everyone in our lives except ourselves. But the good news is that we can choose the ultimate empowerment strategy: cultivating the sacred art of self-nurturing and feeding our resilience, strength, and self-love.

My transformational journey inspired me to write *The Art of Self-Nurturing: A Field Guide To Living With More Peace, Joy, and Meaning* to support women in cultivating empowering self-nurturing practices. I am honored to teach The Art of Self-Nurturing workshops to organizations committed to improving the world and encouraging educators, counselors, therapists, case managers, nurses, social workers, and leaders to embrace the life-changing practice of self-nurturing.

We can become beacons of love and light in a world that dearly needs it, starting by loving ourselves. We can nurture our most radiant inner sparkle and ignite healing and transformation in the world.

We are the ones we have been waiting for.

Shine brightly, dear ones!
"I AM JOYFULLY RESILIENT."
By Kelley Grimes

KELLEY GRIMES, MSW BIOGRAPHY

Kelley Grimes, MSW, is an empowering counselor, self-nurturing expert, sought-after speaker and workshop facilitator, and best-selling author of *The Art of Self-Nurturing: A Field Guide To Living With More Peace, Joy, and Meaning*. She is the founder of Cultivating Peace and Joy, empowering individuals to nurture peace, love, and compassion in the world from the inside out.

Kelley is passionate about inspiring overwhelmed and exhausted individuals to live with more peace, joy, and meaning through the practice of self-nurturing. She also provides professional and leadership development to organizations dedicated to making the world a better place.

In addition, Kelley teaches self-nurturing practices and strategies to women overcoming adversity for Leap to Success, where she serves as a senior director, instructor, and leadership coach. She also loves supervising the social work team and mentoring Master of Social Work interns at the Epilepsy Foundation. Kelley lives in Carlsbad, California, in a four-generational household, is married to an artist and board game maker, and loves playing with her adorable grandchildren, traveling, painting, and singing with a small women's group.

CONNECT WITH KELLEY:

Website: www.cultivatingpeaceandjoy.com
Follow on Socials: IG @cultivatingpeaceandjoy, FB @ CultivatingPeaceAndJoy
#Counselor #Author #Speaker #Workshop Facilitator #SelfNurturing

CHAPTER 11

RISING IN HOLLYWOOD: PERSEVERANCE, PASSION, AND INNER POWER

"You're never too old to say YES to who you are inside."

By Tisha Vaculin

Tisha Vaculin's journey is a testament to the power of perseverance, faith, and an unshakable belief in one's dreams. From a young girl mesmerized by the magic of Hollywood to the powerhouse CEO of Rockefeller Entertainment, her path was anything but easy. Life threw its toughest challenges at her—single motherhood, breast cancer, and battles with depression—but each obstacle became a stepping stone, fueling her determination. With unfiltered honesty, Tisha shares the defining moments that shaped her, revealing how she turned adversity into a force for unstoppable success.

Tisha's story is a testament to the power of never giving up on yourself, no matter how difficult the journey may seem.

RISING IN HOLLYWOOD:
PERSEVERANCE, PASSION, AND INNER POWER

People always say, "Follow your dreams."

For me, it feels like a dream to have done what I've done and become who I am today—the CEO of Rockefeller Entertainment, an award-winning creative studio and production company known for creating premium entertainment experiences, including stage productions, films, and television, with a focus on family-friendly and iconic stories.

It was a long, complicated, and challenging journey, balancing single motherhood, dating, going through breast cancer and depression, and building a successful career in Hollywood. But every struggle, every late night, and every sacrifice was worth it.

When I was four, I told my mom I wanted to be like Shirley Temple. I watched all her shows—though they were old black-and-white movies by then. I saw myself in her. I was obsessed with Shirley Temple. That same year, my mom enrolled me in modeling, where I did runway work and photo shoots. I loved being in front of the camera. It felt like home. I couldn't get enough of it—whether on stage, on set, or anywhere with an audience.

I'll never forget the moment I knew, without a doubt, that I was born to be an actress. I was eight when my mom, her husband, sister, aunt, uncle, three cousins, and I took our first trip to Universal Studios in California. As my mom held my hand, we walked into a large room—at least, it seemed significant to me then. I remember looking around in awe, my eyes landing on a bike with E.T. in the front basket. My heart raced as I realized, "This is where they filmed E.T. This is so cool!"

A group of about thirty to fifty people had gathered, all eager to volunteer for a chance to ride the bike. Without hesitation, I raised my hand and declared, "I'll do it!" *I* wanted to show them how it was done.

They picked me.

I ran to the front, climbed onto the bike, and pedaled. Suddenly, I was soaring across the sky—at least, that's how it looked on the green screen. Watching the crowd react, feeling the thrill of performing, I had a revelation: I was meant for this. At that moment, my destiny aligned with my soul. I knew, with absolute certainty, that I was meant to be an actress. I belonged on stage. I belonged in front of the camera. This wasn't just a childhood fantasy—it was my calling. And I was going to make it happen, not just for the love of acting but to create financial security for myself and my family for generations to come.

But the road wasn't easy.

I was born in Salt Lake City, Utah, and as a child, I was painfully shy—quiet and reserved. Yet, I transformed when it came to dancing, singing, acting, or putting on a show. I became the director, the producer, the actor, and the singer—I was a one-woman show from the moment I could walk. My passion for acting was so intense that I would tell people I was already in movies and TV shows. I even convinced people I was the princess from *The NeverEnding Story.* And you know what? I believed it myself.

In high school, I stayed busy. I was on the swim team, played baseball, competed in pageants, danced, sang, and performed in theater productions. I loved theatrical singing because it allowed endless characterization and expression. Every form of acting had its art and dynamic, and I wanted to master them all.

And so, I kept going. I never stopped chasing the dream because I knew it wasn't just a dream. It was my destiny.

THE EASTER THAT SHAPED MY LIFE

It was early Easter morning. I was eleven, excited for the day's festivities—hunting for eggs and attending church. I couldn't wait any longer, so I rushed into my mom and her husband's bedroom to wake them up. His response was not what I expected. Angrily, he told me to go back to bed. Disappointed, I turned to leave, but before I could stop myself, I sassed back, "If you weren't up partying all night, maybe you'd get up."

That was the wrong thing to say to a hungover man. What happened next would change my life, my sister's, and my mother's forever.

I headed for the bathroom to shower and prepare for Easter. I shut the door, locked it behind me, and stepped into the warm water. As I was washing my hair, a loud thud rattled the door. In an instant, it burst open. He had kicked it down.

Before I could react, he grabbed me by my wet hair, yanked me out of the shower, and beat me. I was naked, terrified, and helpless. All I could do was curl into a ball on the floor, hoping he would stop—or that my mother would save me. Moments later, I heard her pounding on the door, pleading with him to let her in. But instead of stopping, he turned his rage on her. I watched in horror as he struck her hard across the face. She collapsed to the floor, unconscious.

That moment changed everything.

That day, I made a silent vow: I would never marry a man like that. I would never have children. I believed that by not having kids, I could protect them from experiencing the kind of pain I had endured. I also knew I couldn't stay in that town forever. Someday, I would leave.

Mom left him after that. She worked multiple jobs to keep a roof over our heads and food on the table. As the eldest, I took on the caretaker role—for my mom, my sister, and all of us. It was a burden, but I carried it willingly. I loved them deeply, and that experience shaped my identity.

YOUNG LOVE, BIG DREAMS, AND UNEXPECTED TURNS

By the time I was fourteen, I had thrown myself into modeling. It gave me confidence and a sense of control over my life. I was determined to become everything I had dreamed of. At fourteen, I was featured in *Seventeen* magazine, even though I was younger than most models. I traveled to Arizona to work with Ford Models, walking runways and building my portfolio.

From a young age, I used alcohol to silence my anger and numb the pain of childhood trauma. It became my escape; the only way I knew to cope with the memories and heartache—aside from immersing myself in my acting and modeling career.

Then, I met Jack, the love of my life. I was fourteen when we first met. We could talk for hours. He was raised in a strict Mormon family, while I grew up in a Catholic household. My family, especially my mom and grandfather, were more spiritual than religious. My grandfather had a special gift, just like my mother. Despite our different religious backgrounds, Jack and I had an undeniable connection.

At seventeen, I became pregnant. His parents insisted we get married, so we did. We were just kids, completely unprepared for the reality of marriage and parenthood. I was still trying to figure out who I was while also trying to be a wife and mother.

I spent two and a half years working at Advanced Technical Center, a school specializing in Microsoft degrees, of which my mother was part-owner. Math was one of my strengths in school, so I quickly picked up both front-end software and back-end server diagnostics.

Jack joined the military, and we were transferred to Chicago. After living in Chicago for a while, I knew I wanted to transition from modeling to acting. I needed to be in California if I wanted my career to take off. I told Jack my plan, and he got stationed in San Diego, so then we made the move.

When our daughter, Felicia, was about six or eight months old, Jack left. He wanted to "find himself," leaving me alone to raise our baby. I was devastated but determined. I worked at Microsoft as a computer programmer, working twelve-hour shifts to provide for us while acting on the side. I did what my mother had done—worked tirelessly to survive.

A NEW BEGINNING, HEARTBREAK, AND MY BIG BREAK

During this time, our daughter stayed with Jack's parents in Utah while we sorted things out between us. We didn't realize that they did not intend to give her back.

San Diego was everything I had dreamed of for my career—a city full of opportunity, creativity, and the promise of a fresh start. Jack and I made the difficult decision to part ways as a couple but agreed to remain friends, and committed to co-parenting our daughter.

However, his parents saw things differently. They disapproved of my decision to pursue a career while raising a young child, believing a mother's place was solely at home. To them, my aspirations as an actress and model were reckless, irresponsible—even unworthy. They made it their mission to drive a wedge between Jack and me and manipulated the circumstances to gain control.

What began as quiet interference soon escalated into an all-out battle—one that would alter the course of my life forever.

Instead of a custody fight between Jack and me, we found ourselves united against his parents. They were relentless, determined to take Felicia from us. We fought with everything we had, but the legal system drained us emotionally, financially, and spiritually. In the end, it wasn't enough.

We lost. Our precious daughter was taken from us, and with her, a piece of my soul.

She was my world and losing her shattered me. I was devastated, not just by the court's decision, but by what felt like a betrayal from God Himself. I had believed He could intervene, that He could stop it—but He didn't. That was when my faith crumbled. It wasn't just my marriage or my idea of family that broke that day. My trust in Him did, too.

Healing my relationship with my daughter has been a long journey. Even now, as adults, we are still working to rebuild what was lost. But I hold onto gratitude—for the time we have now and the love that still connects us.

In 1999, while living in San Diego, acting opportunities differed from today. You had to attend auditions in person without Zoom or digital options. One of my first auditions was for a small role in a movie with Diane Keaton. I didn't have a single line, but I was thrilled to be in a scene with her.

Then came my big break. My agent encouraged me to audition for a pilot show. Around the same time, I was offered a role in a film with Arnold Schwarzenegger. My agent advised me that it was unlikely that the pilot would succeed, so I took the movie role with Arnold instead.

The pilot? *Lost.*

I learned a valuable lesson—*never assume something won't be life-changing just because it's unfamiliar. Sometimes, you have to take a chance.*

That lesson has shaped my career and my life. Today, as the CEO of Rockefeller Entertainment, I carry that wisdom with me.

Life is full of unexpected turns; immense opportunities often come disguised as the slightest chances.

A SECOND BLESSING

I prayed endlessly for the pain to stop—the agony of losing my daughter and the weight of childhood trauma that I had never confronted. I was lost, drowning in sorrow, unsure of what I wanted from life. Each night, I cried myself to sleep, numbing the ache with alcohol. I showed up on set drunk, miserable, and spiraling out of control. I wanted to stop drinking and to stop showing up to work intoxicated, but I didn't know how to exist without it.

For years, I was furious with God. I blamed Him for everything I had lost. But when I could no longer bear the burden, I surrendered. With a broken heart, I finally asked Him for help.

And He answered.

I remember the day Jack called. He had a three-day leave from the military and wanted to stay with me. Though we were divorced, we had remained friends. I still loved him, and a part of me always wished things had worked out differently. The moment I picked him up from the airport, my heart melted. For a brief time, we found our way back to each other, sharing a beautiful moment of love and connection. For the first time in a long time, I felt happy.

A few months later, I discovered I was pregnant with our second daughter, Katie.

God had blessed me with another chance—with a beautiful child I would raise on my own. I needed her more than I could put into words. Losing Felicia, our first daughter, had shattered me, but Katie became my light. Felicia had taught me the meaning of unconditional love from the moment she was born. In her way, Katie gave me something I hadn't felt in years—peace.

With her, I finally began to heal. I stopped drinking and felt God's presence back in my life. I was happy again. I earned my Microsoft Certified Systems Engineer (MCSE) degree during my pregnancy with Katie. I remember sitting in class, surrounded mainly by intelligent men, with a trash can next to me, throwing up from morning sickness. I asked my instructor if I could take the Transmission Control Protocol/Internet Protocol (TCP/IP) test first, knowing my confidence would falter if others failed before me. He agreed, and I became the first in my class to take and pass the test..

REDEFINING LOVE, CAREER, AND MOTHERHOOD

When Katie was three and a half years old, we lived in Los Angeles. One night, while filming a movie at a nightclub in Utah, I met the owner, Tim. What started as a few phone calls soon turned into deeper conversations, and when we finally met in person, everything moved quickly. Two months later, I found out I was pregnant.

We decided to get married, and soon after, we moved to Las Vegas—a middle ground between Utah and Los Angeles, where we hoped to build our new life together.

Even though we had never really dated, I remember thinking, "This isn't possible."

After Katie, I had been told I wouldn't be able to have more children. It felt unreal—unexpected. At the time, I didn't see it as a blessing, but looking back, I know now it was another gift from God.

I had just been cast as briefcase girl number fifteen on *Deal or No Deal;* a role with a $200,000-per-episode contract. Walking away from that opportunity devastated me. Acting had always been my dream, my purpose, and now I was pregnant. *God, is this a joke?* I thought.

Then, I found out I was having a boy. My heart swelled excitedly when the words left the doctor's lips—I had always wanted a son. When he was born, the nurses lifted him so I could see him before taking him away to be cleaned, and in that instant, he smiled at me. It was a moment I would never forget.

After Ayeden's birth, I tried to continue my acting career, but Tim's jealousy became an obstacle. He was furious when I mentioned a kissing scene in an upcoming role. Over time, he convinced me to walk away from those opportunities. I resented it—hadn't I worked my whole life for this? But stepping away from acting led me down an unexpected path. I learned how to produce, secure funding, and work behind the scenes. My career evolved, and I earned my first producer and executive producer credits. It was a blessing in disguise.

Ironically, just as my career flourished, my marriage unraveled. Tim's unresolved childhood trauma manifested as emotional and mental abuse. Looking back, I believe he did the best he could, but his pain became my burden.

Now, with time and wisdom, I understand. God brought these men into my life to teach me a powerful truth: I am worthy of love, respect, and a partner who isn't threatened by my strength.

THE REALITY OF SINGLE MOTHERHOOD

After my divorce from Tim, I faced the immense challenge of raising two children alone. Custody battles and ongoing disagreements with Tim eventually led me to relocate to Sacramento, California, where I lived just down the street from him.

Financially, those years were an uphill battle. As the sole provider for my kids, I constantly struggled to make ends meet. Paying rent each month was a relentless source of stress, often requiring me to negotiate with landlords to keep a roof over our heads. My mom had instilled in me two essential rules: always pay your rent and always make your car payment—because without a home and transportation, everything else crumbles. I held onto that advice like a lifeline.

Through it all, my children were my driving force. More than anything, I wanted them to have two things: a stable home and nourishing meals. No matter how tight money was, I made sure we lived in good neighborhoods—sometimes ones I couldn't even afford—because I was determined to protect them from the struggles I endured growing up. As a child, I lived on the wrong side of the tracks, where my skin color made me a target. The hardship strengthened me, but I didn't want my kids to experience it.

NAVIGATING LOVE AS A SINGLE MOM

Dating as a single mom was complicated, especially while trying to build a career. I met some great guys, but the relationships were always short-lived; nothing seemed to go anywhere. I used to brush off the idea that having kids would make dating harder. People would say, "Men don't want to date a woman with children," and I thought that was ridiculous. But over time, I realized there was some truth to it.

Successful men often wanted to build their own families, not join an existing one. I'd hear, "You're amazing, but I want to start fresh."

I knew my worth, but to them, I was baggage.

Men were drawn to my confidence and success—at first. But once they saw my life as an actress and TikTok influencer, admiration turned to jealousy, and control soon followed.

For a long time, I stayed single—until Tom.

Tom was my best friend for four years. Being 1,200 miles apart, we built a connection through long conversations, believing we truly knew each other. But distance can hide a lot. When we finally met in person and spent real time together, I discovered the painful truth—he was an alcoholic, hiding his struggles from me all along. Having overcome my battle with drinking, I knew I couldn't be in that environment again.

BREAKING THE CYCLE: OVERCOMING DEPRESSION AND BREAST CANCER

During my on-again, off-again relationship with Tom, I found myself consumed by something far more destructive than love; I was losing myself. Depression crept in slowly at first until it became unbearable.

Once again, I neglected myself, prioritizing a man's pain over my own. I loved Tom, but his struggles pulled me under—a cycle I had repeated for years, giving until I had nothing left.

Depression took me to a dark place, to a terrifying edge where I questioned if I even wanted to keep going. The weight of everything felt suffocating, and I nearly lost myself to it. But by the grace of God—and the unwavering love of my close friends and family—I was talked off that ledge.

Then came a life-changing moment—I found a lump in my breast. The diagnosis was precise, and I made the difficult decision to remove both the lump and my implants. As an actress and model, my appearance had shaped my identity and letting that go felt like losing a part of myself.

But as I stood at that crossroads, something inside me shifted. I realized that my identity wasn't tied to my body—it was tied to the woman I was becoming. No longer just an actress or a model, I was evolving into a professional woman, working as the CEO of Rockefeller Entertainment. More importantly, I was learning to redefine my worth on my terms.

The universe was forcing me to wake up with my diagnosis of breast cancer. I realized that for far too long, I had prioritized everyone else over myself. Battling depression and breast cancer made me realize that to survive—physically, emotionally, and spiritually—I had to put myself first and deepen my faith.

And I'm still learning how to do that every single day.

STANDING IN FAITH: EMBRACING MY POWER AND PURPOSE

God has always been a part of my life. Even when I strayed, lost in the chaos of Hollywood or the pain of my past, He never left me. I know I can always grow deeper in my faith, and as I continue to evolve in my business and personal life, I see His presence guiding me in ways I never did before.

A significant shift in my journey was learning discernment—especially in Hollywood. In my twenties, I prioritized connections over character, seeing fame as a stepping-stone. But now, I'm wiser. I surround myself with those who align with my values, uplift me, and share my faith. This clarity came through growth, hard lessons, and years of hardship.

The most beautiful part?

I see God's hand in everything I'm attracting.

The people I work with, the community I've built, we sometimes pray before filming. And when it happens, I feel a sense of alignment and purpose I have never experienced.

I'm grateful for what I've built in Hollywood; proud that I stayed true to myself and accomplished my dream of becoming a successful actress, starring in a movie at Universal Studios, and standing where my childhood dream began with *E.T.* Not many people can say they achieved what they set out to do, *but I can.*

Today, I am building generational wealth and creating a legacy for my children to carry forward. As young adults, my three children are actively contributing to the growth of my entertainment company, using the gifts and talents they've developed over the years.

And now, as I look ahead, I feel open—open to love, new possibilities, and the next chapter that God has in store for me. This time, I know my worth: a man who truly sees me, embraces my strength rather than fears it, and supports and cherishes me for exactly who I am.

Only God knows what's next, and I trust His plan completely.

I've embraced my journey and learned from life's challenges, and now I'm stepping into my light and inner sparkle.

Join me. Let's step into the light together and shine our inner sparkle.
"I AM HER."
By Tisha Vaculin

TISHA VACULIN BIOGRAPHY

In the world of entertainment, few stars captivate like Tisha Vaculin. With a career spanning over three decades, Vaculin has made her mark on both film and television, enchanting audiences with her versatility and dedication. Her journey began in 1993, with a victory in *Seventeen Magazine's* model contest, a launchpad that led to a dynamic and enduring career in front of the camera. Today, Vaculin is celebrated for her standout role in *I Really Hate My Ex* and her fourteen-episode run on *Fashion House*, as well as her beloved appearances in Disney Channel classics *Return to Halloweentown* and *High School Musical.*

Beyond her impressive acting portfolio, Vaculin draws inspiration from her mentor, Troy Byer, and admires Reese Witherspoon as a model of the accomplished, compassionate woman she aspires to be. Off-screen, Vaculin finds balance through her love for nature, swimming with seals in Mexico, giving back, and always seeking ways to uplift others and make a positive impact.

Vaculin's philosophy on style is simple: Embrace your individuality. For her, confidence is the secret ingredient to any unforgettable look. Despite a busy life, she prioritizes fitness, hitting the gym seven days a week, and surrounding herself with encouraging friends. Her exciting projects include a supporting role in the upcoming film *Stem*, set to begin filming in mid-2025, and her recent promotion to CEO of R.C. Rockefeller Entertainment. She leaves us with advice to live by: "This is your life. Love yourself and embrace what you've been given. Follow your dreams and take that trip you've been saying you want to take."

CONNECT WITH TISHA:

Follow on Social: IG @Tisha.vaculin, TT @tishavaculin1

CHAPTER 12

HONORING THE SACRED JOURNEY OF SELF-LOVE

"Self-love isn't a destination. It's a journey."

By Bobbi Wilcox

In this heartfelt story of "Honoring The Sacred Journey of Self-Love," Bobbi Wilcox takes readers through a transformative moment in her life, where she stood at a crossroads and faced an undeniable emptiness beneath the surface of her seemingly happy marriage. After a crumbling marriage and facing personal turmoil, Bobbi began to uncover the importance of self-love. Through moments of deep reflection, spiritual awakening, and painful decisions, she realized that healing and transformation could only start when she chose to love and honor herself.

With courage and faith, Bobbi rebuilt her life from the inside out, discovering that self-love is not only essential for personal growth but is the foundation for true inner peace and joy. This chapter is a moving exploration of how embracing self-love can lead to profound healing and a deeper connection with one's loving essence.

HONORING THE SACRED JOURNEY OF SELF-LOVE

STANDING AT A CROSSROADS

It was 1998, on a beautiful spring day in Las Vegas, Nevada. My husband at the time, our two young children, and I called this city home. Spring in the desert had always been my favorite—a season of possibilities before the summer heat took over. That day, as I left my office early to pick up groceries before collecting the kids, I reflected on my life.

I ran my own vehicle registration business then, sparing people the agony of long DMV lines. On the surface, my life seemed full—I had a thriving business, a happy family, and the occasional vacation. But underneath, I felt an undeniable void.

As I wandered up and down the aisles at the grocery store, my thoughts drifted to a trip we'd taken to to Kona on the Big Island of Hawaii. The kids laughed joyfully as we built sandcastles under the golden sun and snorkeled in the clear blue water. Yet, that trip also marked the moment I fully realized my marriage was crumbling. A vicious argument with my husband, who threatened to move to a separate hotel room for the rest of the vacation, interrupted our family fun time together.

Despite the laughter and beauty, I couldn't escape the truth: infidelity, lies, and constant conflict had eroded the foundation of our relationship. I had been running on empty, pretending a successful business could fill the growing emotional void. My marriage was falling apart, and deep down, I knew I had been in denial for far too long. I'd even stopped praying, unlike the faith-filled child I once was. At just five years old, I'd given my heart to Jesus, inspired by my grandmother's unwavering faith, which taught me how to have a personal relationship with God. How had I strayed so far from that childlike trust?

Standing in the grocery store aisle, the world's weight came crashing down. Anger and despair bubbled to the surface as I silently cried out, "Is this all there is to my life, God?"

That cry of my soul was a turning point. I realized my life would remain unchanged unless I chose to change it. Though no immediate answers came, a profound peace washed over me. It was God assuring me that I would be okay and reminding me to trust and wait for His divine direction.

In that difficult season, I recognized that I was searching for more than just a way out of my circumstances—I was seeking the light. I opened my heart and asked for Divine help to guide me out of the darkness, and in doing so, I began to rediscover the faith I thought I had lost. Although it wasn't a solution, it was the beginning—a quiet invitation to step onto a new path. A journey of rediscovering faith, reclaiming self-worth, and learning to love myself.

I've understood that certain moments—and even entire decades—can become pivotal in a woman's life, revealing deep-seated beliefs we've unknowingly carried for years. In that season of my life, I uncovered one of the most transformative beliefs about myself:

Self-love is essential!

UNPACKING SELF-LOVE

Growing up, I misunderstood self-love. I'd been taught to prioritize others, believing it was selfish to focus on myself. The biblical teaching, "Love your neighbor as yourself," seemed to reinforce this idea. As a child, I thought this meant I had to sacrifice my own needs to earn love and approval. This belief shaped my relationships, leading me to become a 'people-pleaser.'

In my first marriage, this pattern left me trapped in a cycle of emotional and verbal abuse. I lived to please my husband, neglecting my own happiness and feeling guilty for wanting even the smallest gestures of attention, appreciation, or respect, all the while losing sight of who I was. I believed that prioritizing myself was selfish, wrong, and that I was undeserving, without knowing my worth. Over time, my inner light dimmed, and I no longer recognized the vibrant, confident woman I had once been. My soul cried out for change, and I came to a life-altering realization: for the sake of my survival and my future, I had to leave an unhealthy relationship. Something within me—a flicker of courage—refused to give up. Removing myself from the relationship became my first act of self-love.

THE PAINFUL PATH TO HEALING

Walking away wasn't easy—it was one of my hardest decisions. It came with fear, countless trials, and self-doubt. For years, I had known my marriage was unhealthy, but I didn't know how to leave or where to find the courage to begin again.

Divorce was excruciating, especially with children involved. It brought challenges, grief, and the harsh reality of co-parenting. I wrestled with feelings of failure and inadequacy, cycling through denial, anger, and loneliness. It was undeniably painful, yet healing began to take root amid the darkness. I learned invaluable lessons about myself. I realized that continuing on the same path would only lead to the same outcomes. The definition of insanity is doing the same thing repeatedly and expecting different results. The change I needed to make had to start within me. Slowly, I rediscovered my strength and confidence and realized that my worth wasn't tied to my marital status or anyone else's approval. This newfound understanding became a foundation for my journey to self-love.

Looking back, I now see that choosing to leave a relationship that no longer served my highest good, emotional, mental, or spiritual, was a profound act of self-love and a response to my soul's cry for help. It was also an act of courage. The biblical verse "Love your neighbor as yourself" (Mark 12:31 NIV) took on a whole new meaning for me. I understood that we can only love others as deeply as we love ourselves. If I don't care for, honor, respect, or value myself, how can I offer those things to anyone else? Loving myself wasn't selfish; it was necessary.

FINDING THE TOOLS FOR TRANSFORMATION

Spirit led me to the University of Santa Monica, where I studied spiritual psychology from 2002 to 2004. These years were transformative. I learned the art of heart-centered listening and began to see myself through the lens of unconditional love. Heart-centered listening—listening with love and compassion and without judgment—and how to recognize the loving essence within me and others shifted my awareness in profound ways. As I listened to another valuable human being from my heart and not my head, I began to experience unconditional love and understanding for them and myself.

This work was deeply personal and often painful, because I learned to confront limiting beliefs that had kept me small:

"I'm a terrible mom for abandoning my kids."

"I'm not capable of making it on my own."

"I'm not good enough, smart enough, thin enough, or confident enough."

Slowly, I started dismantling those beliefs and replacing them with a deeper understanding of my inherent worth.

Have you ever felt trapped by such beliefs? What stories do you tell yourself about who you are?

I learned that acceptance is the first step toward change. I accept that I cannot change others; I can only change myself. For years, I tried to change my husband (wasband or ex-husband). What was I thinking? If you've ever been through a divorce, maybe you can relate. Trying to change someone is not only challenging but also impossible.

What I came to realize is that *it wasn't the pain of divorce that defined me—it was the healing that came afterward.*

That journey of growth reshaped me, both personally and spiritually. Slowly but surely, I emerged stronger, wiser, more confident, compassionate, and self-loving. I was transformed from the inside out, and my inner light began to SPARKLE again.

IDENTIFYING LIMITING BELIEFS

One of the most profound shifts in my self-love journey came when I uncovered a core belief: I was unworthy of love. This belief had fueled jealousy and insecurity, creating unnecessary pain in my relationship with my first husband. If he so much as looked at or talked to another woman, I would automatically assume he was cheating on me. I'd become outraged and feel completely unable to trust him. Beneath the anger, though, was a deep hurt that consumed me. I couldn't sleep, eat, or function without obsessively worrying about him being unfaithful. This was no way to live.

Back then, I didn't understand my self-worth. The concept was entirely foreign to me. It wasn't until I attended USM that I began learning to identify and release limiting beliefs through self-awareness and forgiveness. I learned to approach emotions like anger or sadness as invitations to dig deeper. I asked myself questions such as:

- What thoughts did I have that were tied to this emotion or feeling?
- How do I feel about the situation?
- What belief might be fueling these feelings?

Through reflection, I discovered that my jealousy and insecurity weren't really about my husband at all. They were about me—my feelings of unworthiness. As tricky as this realization was, it was also liberating. I could change the story I was telling myself.

What about you? Is there a limiting belief you've been holding onto? Take a moment to reflect. Could you replace it with an empowering truth? How might your life change if you did?

For me, replacing limiting beliefs with empowering ones became a daily practice. I started with affirmations like, "I am worthy. I am lovable. I am enough."

At first, these words felt awkward and untrue, but they began to resonate with me over time. Whenever I felt upset, I asked myself more profound questions, uncovering the root of my emotions.

This practice taught me that *no one else has the power to make me feel happy or upset—that power lies within me.*

Whenever I feel triggered by someone's actions or words, I ask myself, "What inside me feels this way?" This question became the starting point for transformation.

Today, I live by a new belief: *loving myself isn't just okay, it's essential.*

Self-love is healthy, empowering, and transformative. It's the foundation for loving myself and others authentically.

SELF-FORGIVENESS: A PATH TO FREEDOM

Like many, I grew up learning the importance of forgiving others, but forgiving myself? That wasn't in my consciousness. It wasn't until I learned about compassionate self-forgiveness that everything changed. For years, I carried the weight of harsh self-judgments:

"I'm a terrible mom."

"I'm an unlovable wife."

"I'm not enough."

These thoughts played on repeat, eating away at my sense of worth. At its core, compassionate self-forgiveness addresses judgment—the root of our emotional suffering. It stems from the belief that we're not enough. Judgment sneaks in when we condemn ourselves, often without even realizing it. These beliefs reinforced my feelings of inadequacy and kept me trapped in a cycle of self-blame and suffering.

One moment stands out vividly. I was in a class at the University of Santa Monica where we practiced compassionate self-forgiveness. Sitting down, I noticed a classmate resembling my wasband's girlfriend. The resemblance was uncanny, and I was immediately triggered.

I felt my heart start to beat faster. All of the hurt and anger I thought I'd buried came rushing back. I had blamed her for the collapse of my marriage. I believed she had stolen my husband, torn apart my family, and ruined my life. And as much as I wanted to move on, I also wanted to hate her. I thought holding onto that anger gave me some upper hand.

That day, as part of the exercise, I was asked to share a time when I felt hurt or upset. I took a deep breath and began. "I'm here to heal from my divorce," I said, my voice trembling. "My wasband and I were unfaithful to one another. For years, we denied it, and nothing changed. I stayed because I didn't know how to support myself or my kids without him. And in staying, I allowed everything to stay the same."

My classmate, acting as the counselor, listened patiently. "That sounds incredibly painful," she said gently. "I hear how betrayed you felt and how much you were carrying."

As I spoke, I became aware of how much pain and judgment I had been carrying—toward the girlfriend, my husband, and myself. I had seen her as controlling, held onto the hurt my husband caused, and blamed myself for not leaving sooner. I judged everything—and it was overwhelming.

I was guided to close my eyes, place my hands over my heart, and speak compassionately to myself. I started slow, feeling the resistance in my heart. But as the words came, something began to shift:

I forgive myself for judging her as manipulative.
I forgive myself for believing she stole my husband and family.
I forgive myself for hating her.
I forgive myself for holding onto this pain for so long.
I forgive myself for judging myself as weak for not leaving.

The words felt strange initially, but tears started streaming down my face as I repeated them. It was as if a dam had broken inside me. The more I forgave, the lighter I felt.

Then came the truth—my truth:

I am a loving and worthy person.
I was doing the best I could with what I knew at the time.
I am enough, just as I am.

Something powerful shifted in me that day. Forgiving the girlfriend, myself, and my wasband wasn't about condoning what had happened or for getting the pain. It was about freeing myself. For the first time, I understood that forgiveness is a choice, not a feeling. And forgiving myself for the judgments I had carried was the key to unlocking my heart.

My spiritual teachers, Drs. Ron and Mary Hulnick, often say, *"Healing is the application of loving."*

And they're right. That day, I applied love to the most wounded parts of myself; the parts that had been buried under years of hurt and blame.

Compassionate self-forgiveness is tender, like comforting a child who's been hurt. It's saying *I see your pain and love you anyway.* It's reconnecting with the love within you and offering it to yourself.

This practice didn't heal me overnight, but I felt a little freer every time I forgave myself. The weight of judgment lifted slowly, making space for peace, joy, and love.

If you've ever felt trapped by anger, guilt, and pain, especially after a divorce, you're not alone.

I know how heavy it feels. But compassionate self-forgiveness can break those chains. It's not about forgetting or excusing; it's about choosing to love yourself enough to let go. And in that letting go, you'll find freedom.

LOVING SELF-CARE

Self-care became my gateway to self-love—a way to honor every part of me: body, mind, emotions, and spirit. But it wasn't always that way.

Before attending the University of Santa Monica, I thought I had self-care figured out. I exercised, ate well, prayed, and stayed active in church. Yet, something was missing. My self-care was surface-level, and I hadn't learned how to truly nurture my emotions or connect with myself on a deeper spiritual level.

That changed during my first year at the university. One moment that stood out was a simple grocery shopping trip with friends at Whole Foods. I wasn't just learning about healthy eating; I was discovering how to listen to my body. I started choosing foods intentionally, paying attention to what fueled me, like proteins for my O-positive blood type, and avoiding what drained me, like refined sugars. Movement became a gift instead of a chore, and I began walking, stretching, and exercising joyfully.

But the fundamental transformation happened when I turned inward. I started meditating—not just to quiet my mind but to be present with myself. I gave myself permission to feel my emotions fully—grief, anger, joy, or vulnerability—without judgment. Instead of running from them, I let them flow. In doing so, I found freedom.

The most profound shift came when I learned heart-centered listening. It is a spiritual practice of tuning into my inner voice, intuition, and Spirit's guidance. By listening with love, I discovered that self-care wasn't about routines or tasks—it was about seeing myself with compassion and treating myself with the kindness I deserved.

Loving self-care became more than a spiritual practice; it became an act of devotion that I still practice today. I learned to honor my body as a temple, my emotions as sacred messengers, and my spirit as the divine essence of who I am.

This journey taught me that self-care isn't one-size-fits-all or static. It evolves as we do. When we approach it with intention and love, it transforms us and how we show up in the world.

THE POWER OF SELF-LOVE: BUILDING A SACRED RELATIONSHIP WITH YOURSELF

I've come to understand that self-love is about cultivating a sacred relationship with yourself. We spend so much of our lives nurturing relationships with others—parents, children, friends, partners— but how often do we turn inward to tend to our relationship with ourselves?

I remember asking a friend what self-love meant to her. She smiled and said, "It's about spending quiet time in meditation."

Her answer was simple yet profound, reminding me that self-love isn't one-size-fits-all. It's personal, unique, and deeply individual.

For me, *self-love has been a journey of discovery, learning how to nurture myself with the same care and attention I give others. It's about listening to my inner dialogue and recognizing when my ego's critical voice drowns out the gentle whispers of my soul. It's about tuning in to my dreams and desires, noticing moments of clarity and inspiration, and honoring my boundaries without guilt.*

Building a relationship with myself means curiosity about what I need and want. It's about asking myself questions I used to reserve for others:

"What brings me joy?"

"What drains my energy?"

"What do I need right now to take care of me?"

And then, it's about actually listening to and honoring the answers.

Self-love also means forgiving myself for the times I've fallen short, choosing compassion instead of judgment. It's about treating myself with the same tenderness I'd offer a dear friend struggling. It's giving me grace.

Some days, loving myself means nourishing my body with a healthy meal or taking a long walk in the mountains. On other days, it means permitting myself to rest, say "no," or let go of unrealistic expectations. It means recognizing that self-love is not a list of tasks to check off but an ongoing dialogue; a sacred dance of growth, healing, and grace.

What I've come to realize is that this relationship with myself is the foundation of everything else. When I show up for myself with love and care, I feel more aligned, more at peace, and more connected to the truth of who I am: a valuable, worthy, and deeply loved being.

This sacred relationship with myself also strengthens my relationships with others. When I'm grounded in love, I can love others without losing myself. I can set boundaries without guilt and give freely without resentment. Loving myself allows me to bring my full, authentic self into the world.

So, I invite you to ask yourself: *"What would it look like to love and care for myself the way I care for those I love?"*

This is the heart of self-love—showing up for yourself daily with patience, kindness, and an open heart.

Self-love is not a destination. It's a journey—a sacred and lifelong relationship that evolves as you do.

And as you tend to this relationship, you'll discover something beautiful: the more you love yourself, the more you remember the truth of who you are—whole, worthy, and endlessly deserving of love.

LOVING ME WHILE LOVING MY PARTNER

I met my second husband during my second year at the University of Spiritual Psychology. It was winter break, and I was living in Boulder, Colorado, flying back and forth to Los Angeles every month to complete my master's program. The travel was exhausting, but I was committed to finishing my studies.

I was working with my business partner on a groundbreaking technology involving liquid crystals at the time. We had partnered with a professor at the University of Colorado, and long days were our norm. One evening, I decided to treat the office staff to dinner at a cozy sushi spot on Boulder's famous Pearl Street.

As we settled into the restaurant, I noticed a tall, good-looking man with hazel eyes and an easy smile walking toward us. He introduced himself as the restaurant manager and offered us a round of shots on the house. While I politely declined, my team enthusiastically accepted. Throughout the evening, he and I exchanged glances, and I couldn't deny that something about him intrigued me.

At the end of dinner, one of the young women on my staff encouraged me to ask him out. Feeling old-fashioned, I refused, but she had other plans. She marched over to him and told him I was new in town and needed someone to show me around. When she returned, she said, "He said, 'Oh, okay,'" which wasn't exactly the response I'd hoped for.

As we left, the same staff member insisted I go last, saying it would give him another chance to approach me. To my surprise, as I walked out the door, he stopped me and asked for my business card. We exchanged cards, and that simple moment began our story.

Our relationship blossomed and we fell in love. During our time together, I realized he had a high tolerance for drinking—something I didn't share. I was faced with a choice: address the issue or stay silent.

I discussed my concern with him, expressing how I loved him deeply, but I also loved myself enough to know I couldn't live a life where a tolerance for alcohol played a central role in our relationship. I wasn't asking him to change for me; I told him the decision was his alone, not my ultimatum. Later, I realized I was setting a boundary, a lesson I had learned from my first marriage.

He listened. Over time, he made the choice to quit drinking and smoking, left the restaurant industry, and began prioritizing his health and our future together. Two years later, we got married.

Our marriage hasn't been without its challenges—no relationship is—but each one has deepened our connection and helped us grow. We've both made mistakes along the way—he has his, and I certainly have mine—but we've continued to choose love, grace, and each other. Through it all, we've built a foundation of mutual respect, unwavering love, and a shared commitment to personal growth. Through this journey, I've learned one of the most profound lessons: *self-love is the foundation of a healthy, thriving partnership.*

Loving myself while loving him has been an ongoing process. I've learned to set boundaries with grace, speak my truth with courage, and honor my own needs without guilt. I've come to understand that I am worthy of love, respect, and kindness—not just from my husband but from myself. This awareness has deepened my joy and transformed how I show up in our relationship. I also understand that he is worthy of love, respect, and kindness—another valuable lesson I learned about relationships.

Today, we share a beautiful life with our seventeen-year-old son and a blended family of two adult children, our son and daughter, our daughter-in-law, and five wonderful grandchildren. In my first book, *Reconciled*, I share how my wasband and I found healing and forgiveness. In time, both of our families came together for a blended family vacation on an Alaskan cruise—a beautiful testament to God's grace and the power of reconciliation. Our family is filled with love, laughter, and growth; a testament to the foundation we've built together in our two decades of marriage.

What I've come to realize is this: *self-love isn't a destination. It's a lifelong journey*, and being in this relationship has taught me more about self-love than I ever imagined.

As poet Rupi Kaur beautifully says, "How you love yourself is how you teach others to love you."

When we love ourselves fully, we create space for authentic

connection, communication, and lasting joy in all our relationships.

Self-love doesn't enhance partnerships—it transforms them. It lays the foundation for a life rooted in love for yourself and others.

One final thought: through prayer, my relationship with the creator, self-reflection, and intentional self-love, I rediscovered the vibrant, confident Bobbi I was always meant to be. The journey was neither easy nor strict, but each step—shedding limiting beliefs and embracing compassionate self-forgiveness—brought me closer to my true loving essence.

Today, I move through life with renewed joy and purpose, shining my light, my inner sparkle, in all that I do as an author, publisher, spiritual coach, community leader, collaborator, connector, wife, mother, Memaw, daughter, and friend.

What about you? Are you ready to embrace your journey of self-love?

It begins with a tiny, intentional step, knowing you are worthy, lovable, and enough, just as you are.

Ignite your inner sparkle. Your soul is born to soar.
"I AM THE POWER OF INNER SPARKLE"
By Bobbi Wilcox

BOBBI WILCOX BIOGRAPHY

Driven by her passion to inspire, Bobbi founded Heart & Soul Publishing to give women a voice. She created *The Power of Inner Sparkle: Twelve Inspiring Stories to Ignite Your Heart and Soul*, sharing her self-love journey in her chapter, *Honoring The Sacred Journey of Self-Love*. Bobbi is also a contributing author in the number one international bestseller, *Art of Connection: 365 Days of Abundance Quotes by Entrepreneurs, Business Owners, and Influencers*. Her first book, *Reconciled*, was published in 2016.

With a spiritual psychology and personal development background and over thirty years as a business owner, Bobbi embraces a soul-centered leadership approach. She studied at the University of Santa Monica (USM), ran a spiritual counseling practice for step-couples, and successfully built and sold two businesses.

Bobbi advocates for women's empowerment through organizations like the National Association of Women Business Owners (NAWBO), where she served as the Las Vegas chapter president, and Powerful You! She is also a member of the Southern Colorado Women's Chamber of Commerce (SCWCC), serving on the membership committee and the Network of Outstanding Women.

Bobbi's recent work includes her interview with Jack Canfield about *The Power of Inner Sparkle* and hosting the *Sparkle & Soar* book launch and SCWCC fundraiser. She believes uplifting women creates a powerful ripple effect.

Bobbi was born in Las Vegas and lives in Colorado with her husband, Geoff, and their son. She cherishes time with her three adult children, spouses, five grandchildren, and parents. She also enjoys hiking, skiing, soulful coffee chats, and baking.

CONNECT WITH BOBBI:

Website: www.heartnsoulpublish.com
IG & FB & LI: @bobbiwilcoxsparkle

GRATITUDE

I am deeply grateful to Spirit for the calling, love, and direction throughout this journey. Each day, I asked for assistance, guidance, and support in my self-care, in the writing, and the perfect alignment of everything needed to bring this book to life—from the right co-authors, to the timelines, Foreword, celebrity endorsements, book cover, interior design, publishing, and editing. I am thankful for the patience, grace, and perseverance shown and for the love and guidance that led me to the twelve amazing Sparkle Authors. Thank you, God, for this beautiful and passionate calling.

A heartfelt thank you to my eleven beautiful Sparkle Athors— Andrea, Allison, Angela, Havilah, Judy, Katy, Kelley, Lacey, MaryJo, Tisha, and Virginia. Serving and working alongside each of you has been a joy and privilege. Thank you, Theresa "Tgo" Goss, for writing a soulful Foreword and acknowledging all women's beautiful inner sparkle.

To my loving husband, thank you for your quiet support and for always listening as I share my passion. I also want to give a heartwarming thank you to my family, friends, and colleagues for their unwavering encouragement.

Thank you to my Get Published Now team with Steve Harrison. This book wouldn't have been a success without their dedication, knowledge, and support.

A BIG, thank you to the Sparkle Readers, Barbara Butt, Cynthia K Dohrmann, Wendy Fast, Esbeyde Guzman, Crissy J, Heidi Jeseritz, Connie K Malonson, Laurie Michaels, Tamaris Purvines, Tammi Scott, Tina Swinford, Chrissy Wilcox, Melanie Wilcox, and Shauna Woods, for your time, dedication, and valuable feedback. Your insights helped shape this book into what it is today, and we are forever grateful for your impact.

Thank you to my spirit guides, teachers, and angels who guide, nudge, and protect me.

Are You Ready to Reignite Your Inner Sparkle?

Dear Beautiful Soul,

If the stories in this book stirred something within you . . . If you felt seen, heard, and inspired to step more fully into your light, then this is just the beginning.

I invite you to continue your journey of self-love, soul expression, and inner sparkle with us.

Here's Your Next Step:

Join us in one (or more) of these heart-led offerings created especially for women like you:

Join Our Power of Inner Sparkle Book Club

Have you ever finished a book and wished you could sit in with the author—and other women—who really get it? Whether this book opened something inside of you or simply reminded you of who you truly are, this Power of Inner Sparkle Book Club is your invitation to go deeper . . . together.

It's about embodying the sparkle within you and being witnessed in the process. This is a gathering of women who are ready to deepen their connection to themselves, share their voices, and be truly seen and heard.

Find out more here: www.heartnsoulpublish.com/nextsteps
www.facebook.com/groups/heartnsoulpublishing

SHARE YOUR POWER OF INNER SPARKLE STORY: YOUR VOICE MATTERS. YOUR STORY SHINES.

Have you experienced a moment when your light broke through the darkness? A time when you reclaimed your power, your purpose, or your peace?

We'd love to hear your story.

At Heart & Soul Publishing, we believe that when women share their truth, they help others heal, grow, and awaken as well. Whether it's a whisper of change or a bold transformation, your story is worthy of being seen and heard. Your words may be featured (with your permission) in our community, on social media, or even in a future Heart & Soul Publishing project.

Submit your story at: www.heartnsoulpublish.com/nextsteps

www.ingramcontent.com/pod-product-compliance
Lightning Source LLC
Chambersburg PA
CBHW071736120626
46550CB00002B/540